LETTERHEAD +
LOGO DESIGN 12

ROCKPORT

First published in the United States of America by
Rockport Publishers, a member of
Quayside Publishing Group
100 Cummings Center
Suite 406-L
Beverly, Massachusetts 01915-6101
Telephone: (978) 282-9590
Fax: (978) 283-2742
www.rockpub.com

Library of Congress Control Number available

ISBN-13: 978-1-59253-717-4
ISBN-10: 1-59253-717-0

Digital edition published in 2011
eISBN-13: 978-1-61058-146-2

10 9 8 7 6 5 4 3 2

Design: Oxide Design Co.
Studio Photography: Lightstream

Printed in China

LETTERHEAD +
LOGO DESIGN 12

Oxide Design Co.

BEVERLY MASSACHUSETTS

ROCKPORT PUBLISHERS

CONTENTS

INTRODUCTION

Just now, you picked up this sharply crafted twelfth edition of Rockport Publishers' **Letterhead + Logo Design** series.

As you did, you brushed your fingers over the spot-varnished cover and wondered how Oxide managed to know everything there is to know about letterhead and logo design.

Truth be told, we don't. And while we're proud of our work (on this book and for our clients), we haven't accomplished anything that would necessarily justify that distinction. Honestly, you may be just as qualified as we are to distinguish the great from the not great.

But that's exactly the point. Design speaks to everyone personally. Its effectiveness and ability to captivate hinge on individual interpretation. So, while Oxide had the privilege of authoring this book, it could have just as easily been you.

In this collection, you'll find all kinds of great design—ideas that are appropriate, well executed, and carry a thoughtfulness that will reward a second look.

We've divided the book into twelve stylistic categories, each of which opens with our unanimous favorite in that category. We've also selected a trio of personal favorites—our way of underscoring the capacity of great design to really take hold of an individual imagination.

But throughout the book, our hope is that we've done our homework and selected work that you—an equally discerning judge of design—will find just as effective and captivating as we do. —

JUDGES' SELECTION: PERSONAL FAVORITES

POESPA
PRODUCTIONS

JUDGE   Drew Davies

DESIGN FIRM   Bekaert Visual Design Team
DESIGNERS   Johnny Bekaert
CLIENT   Poespa Productions

GOOGOO
WONDERLAND

JUDGE   Joe Sparano

DESIGN FIRM   Insight Design Communications
DESIGNERS   Tracy Holdeman
CLIENT   GooGoo Wonderland

JUDGE   Adam Torpin

DESIGN FIRM   Stitch Design Co.
DESIGNERS   Amy Pastre
          Courtney Rowson
CLIENT   The James Pond

ANGULAR

Sharp corners and solid colors

Judges' Selection: Best In Category

Kinetic Bouldering Gym is a grass-roots location for the local climbing community and a colorful museum of climbing holds. This logo works well because it evokes the gym's many faceted walls.

DESIGN FIRM Jeremy Slagle Graphic Design   **DESIGNER** Jeremy Slagle   **CLIENT** Kinetic Bouldering Gym

DESIGN FIRM   brandcut
DESIGNERS   Stanislav Levin
CLIENT   Workstreamer

DESIGN FIRM   Bruketa&Zinic OM
ART DIRECTORS   Imelda Ramovic
    Mirel Hadzijusufovic
    Davor Bruketa
    Nikola Zinic
DESIGNERS   Imelda Ramovic
    Mirel Hadzijusufovic
CLIENT   The Kvarner County Tourism Office

DESIGN FIRM   Beast Syndicate
DESIGNER   Jeremy Thompson
CLIENT   Beast Syndicate

DESIGN FIRM   BrandSavvy, Inc.
ART DIRECTOR   Karl Peters
DESIGNERS   Karl Peters
    Marcus Fitzgibbons
CLIENT   West Georgia Health

Daryn Kuipers
Investment Analyst

The Windquest Group
201 Monroe Avenue NW, Suite 500
Grand Rapids, Michigan 49503
TEL   616 459-4500
FAX   616 459-1211
darynk@windquest.com

The Windquest Group
201 Monroe Avenue NW, Suite 500
Grand Rapids, Michigan 49503
616 459-4500

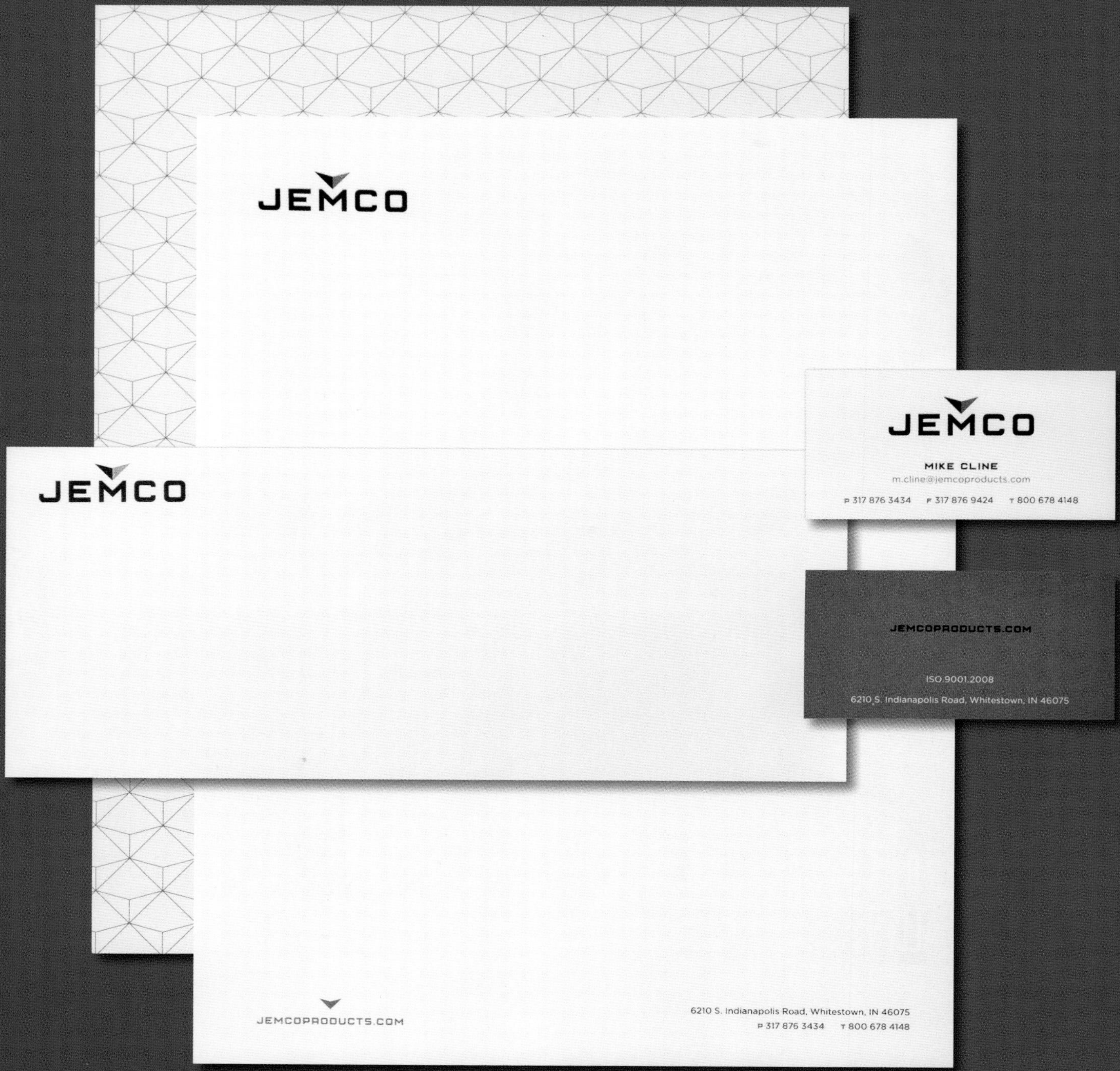

JEMCO

JEMCO

JEMCO

MIKE CLINE
m.cline@jemcoproducts.com
P 317 876 3434   F 317 876 9424   T 800 678 4148

JEMCOPRODUCTS.COM

ISO.9001.2008
6210 S. Indianapolis Road, Whitestown, IN 46075

JEMCOPRODUCTS.COM

6210 S. Indianapolis Road, Whitestown, IN 46075
P 317 876 3434   T 800 678 4148

DESIGN FIRM Miles Design   DESIGNER Amanda Blackburn   CLIENT Jemco Products

DESIGN FIRM   Communication Bureau Proekt
ART DIRECTOR   Roman Krikheli
DESIGNERS   Andrey Koodenko
            Dmitry Rybalkin
CLIENT   Parad boutiques

DESIGN FIRM   Capsule
ART DIRECTOR   Brian Adducci
DESIGNER   Greg Brose
CLIENT   Nolan Properties Group

DESIGN FIRM   Cathy Solarana Design
DESIGNER   Cathy Solarana
CLIENT   Lied Art Gallery at Creighton University

DESIGN FIRM   CAI Communications
DESIGNER   Beth Greene
CLIENT   Association Executives of North Carolina

EXPERTLY ORCHESTRATED GENIUS™

K KEVIN KENNEDY ASSOCIATES™

Kevin Kennedy Associates Inc.
3905 Vincennes Road, Suite 320
Indianapolis, Indiana 46268
317 536 7000 ‹ PH
317 536 7220 ‹ FX
KevinKennedyAssociates.com

K KEVIN KENNEDY ASSOCIATES™

Kevin Kennedy Associates Inc.
3905 Vincennes Road, Suite 320
Indianapolis, Indiana 46268
317 536 7000 ‹ PH
317 536 7220 ‹ FX
KevinKennedyAssociates.com

K KEVIN KENNEDY ASSOCIATES™

Linda Hammer ‹ ACCOUNTING MANAGER

LindaH@KevinKennedyAssociates.com
317 536 7002 ‹ PH
317 429 8002 ‹ FX

EXPERTLY ORCHESTRATED GENIUS™

Kevin Kennedy Associates Inc.
3905 Vincennes Road, Suite 320
Indianapolis, Indiana 46268

KevinKennedyAssociates.com

DESIGN FIRM Miles Design **DESIGNER** Brian K Gray **CLIENT** Kevin Kennedy Associates

KEVIN KENNEDY ASSOCIATES™

Linda Hammer ‹ ACCOUNTING MANAGER

LindaH@KevinKennedyAssociates.com
317 536 7002 ‹ PH
317 429 8002 ‹ FX

DESIGN FIRM EIGA Design
DESIGNER Elisabeth Plass
CLIENT Grafitektur

DESIGN FIRM Flight Deck Creative
DESIGNER Jason Rahn
CLIENT Anita Miller

DESIGN FIRM Flight Deck Creative
DESIGNER Jason Rahn
CLIENT Big Dog Productions

DESIGN FIRM ghost
ART DIRECTOR Matthew Pickett
DESIGNERS Jenkin Hammond
Michael Vidrine
CLIENT Konstruct

DELTA ENTERPRISES

ENTERPRISES

DELTA ENTERPRISES BV | OUDE HAVEN 50 | 4301 CL ZIERIKZEE

DELTA ENTERPRISES

ABE BLIKMAN
MOB   06 251 565 82   •   E-MAIL   ABE@DELTAENTERPRISES.NL

DELTA ENTERPRISES BV   TEL   0111 41 63 49
OUDE HAVEN 50   FAX   0111 41 62 49
4301 CL ZIERIKZEE   E-MAIL INFO@DELTAENTERPRISES.NL

WWW.DELTAENTERPRISES.NL

ENTERPRISES

DELTA ENTERPRISES BV
OUDE HAVEN 50   •   4301 CL   •   ZIERIKZEE   •   TEL. 0111 41 63 49   •   FAX. 0111 41 62 49   •   E-MAIL. INFO@DELTAENTERPRISES.NL
ABN AMRO. 51.45.04.749   •   IBAN. NL76 ABNA 0514 5047 49   •   BIC. ABNANL2A   •   BTW-NUMMER. 005114123B01   •   KVK. 22030666

WWW.DELTAENTERPRISES.NL

OP AL ONZE CONTRACTEN EN OVEREENKOMSTEN ZIJN ONZE ALGEMENE VOORWAARDEN VAN TOEPASSING. DEZE KUNT U VINDEN OP
WWW.DELTAENTERPRISES.NL/ALGEMENEVOORWAARDEN

vision made **real**

CIVIC
COMMERCIAL
HIGHER EDUCATION
INTERIOR DESIGN
K-12 EDUCATION
LANDSCAPE
RESORT / MIXED-USE

MHTN
ARCHITECTS

Bruce M. Haxton, AIA, LEED AP
Senior Project Manager
Design Architect

420 E. South Temple, Ste 100
Salt Lake City, Utah 84111
P 801.595.6700
D 801.326.3270
C 801.633.3532
F 801.326.3370
bruce.haxton@mhtn.com

vision made **real**

420 East South Temple, Suite 100
Salt Lake City, Utah 84111
www.mhtn.com

MHTN
ARCHITECTS

MHTN
ARCHITECTS

420 East South Temple, Suite 100, Salt Lake City, Utah 84111 / P 801.595.6700 / F 801.595.6717 / www.mhtn.com

DESIGN FIRM modern8 **ART DIRECTOR** Randall Smith **DESIGNER** Russ Gray **CLIENT** MHTN Architects

DESIGN FIRM Mirko Ilić Corp.
DESIGNER Mirko Ilić
CLIENT Kvart

DESIGN FIRM Paragon Marketing Communications
DESIGNER Konstantin Assenov
CLIENT 247

DESIGN FIRM People Design
ART DIRECTORS Yang Kim
Kevin Budelmann
DESIGNERS Yang Kim
Josh Best
Neil Hubert
CLIENT Windquest

DESIGN FIRM Yona Lee Design
ART DIRECTORS Yona Lee
Jee-eun Lee
DESIGNER Jee-eun Lee
CLIENT Gallery 64

DESIGN FIRM 5Seven
DESIGNER Clint Delapaz
CLIENT dealnews.com

DESIGN FIRM Ink
CLIENT Koldcast

DESIGN FIRM modern8
ART DIRECTOR Randall Smith
DESIGNER Russ Gray
CLIENT MHTN Architects

DESIGN FIRM Hansen Designs
DESIGNER J. Nathan Hansen
CLIENT Colorado Paint Pros

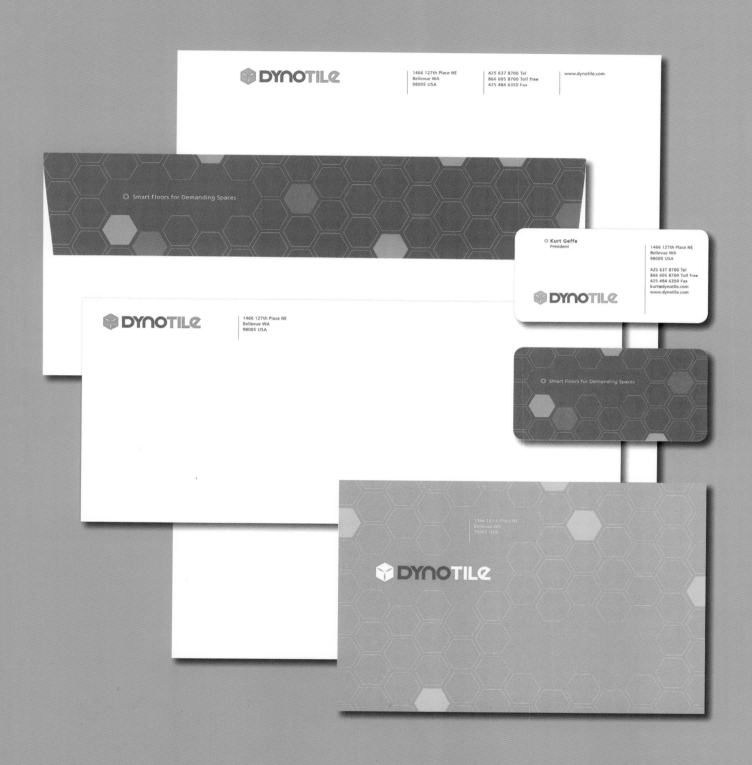

CONCEPTUAL

Designed with thought and purpose

FARE
SHARE
FOOD
BANK

Judges' Selection: Best In Category

Instantly recognizable and understandable, this logo clearly communicates "food bank"
while simultaneously making an allusion to the disconnect between supply and need.

DESIGN FIRM Limelight Advertising & Design   **DESIGNER** Luke Despatie   **CLIENT** Fare Share Food Bank

DESIGN FIRM   A3 Design Inc.
ART DIRECTOR   Amanda Altman
DESIGNERS   Alan Altman
            Rachel Giralico
CLIENT   Carolina Paper

DESIGNER   Alexander Wende
CLIENT   RAWIK LTD.

DESIGN FIRM   brandcut
DESIGNER   Stanislav Levin
CLIENT   Gaucho Wine

DESIGN FIRM   Bronson Ma Creative
DESIGNER   Bronson Ma
CLIENT   Kleckner Consulting

10™

10™

10™

Making brands work since we were 10

Making brands work since we were 10

Making brands work since we were 10

David Worthington

Position
Managing Director

Say hello
david@10associates.co.uk
07989 585049

10 Associates Ltd
Brand & Design

Home
6a Cartwright Court, Bradley Business Park
Dyson Wood Way, Huddersfield HD2 1GN

Tel
01484 543905

Fax
01484 541827

Say hello
hello@10associates.co.uk

Web
www.10associates.co.uk

10 Associates Ltd
Brand & Design

Home
6a Cartwright Court, Bradley Business Park
Dyson Wood Way, Huddersfield HD2 1GN

Tel
01484 543905

Fax
01484 541827

Say hello
hello@10associates.co.uk

Web
www.10associates.co.uk

registered in England 5016398

LADDER ^{up}
FINANCIAL LIBERATION

P.O. BOX 061110
CHICAGO IL 60606-1110

312.466.0771 TEL
312.466.0772 FAX

GOLADDERUP.ORG

AMALIA TURKEWITZ
PROGRAM ASSOCIATE

ATURKEWITZ@GOLADDERUP.ORG

233 S WACKER DRIVE, SUITE 9100
CHICAGO IL 60606-6332

T 312.466.0771 : F 312.466.0772

LADDER ^{up}
FINANCIAL LIBERATION

233 S WACKER DRIVE, SUITE 9100
CHICAGO IL 60606-6332

T 312.466.0771
F 312.466.0772

GOLADDERUP.ORG

ONE FOR YOU.
www.goladderup.org

ONE TO SHARE.
www.goladderup.org

2,900%
RETURN ON
YOUR DONATION.
WE'RE EXACTLY WHO YOU
WANT TEACHING
PEOPLE ABOUT MONEY.

FOR EVERY $1 DONATED TO US, $29 IS REFUNDED TO THE COMMUNITY. THAT'S A 2,900%
RETURN ON YOUR DONATION. MAKE YOUR MONEY MAKE A DIFFERENCE. HELP LOW-INCOME
FAMILIES CLIMB THE ECONOMIC LADDER. FIND OUT MORE AT GOLADDERUP.ORG

LADDER ^{up}
FINANCIAL LIBERATION

DESIGN FIRM Bagby & Co.   **ART DIRECTORS** Nicole Ziegler, Andy Mamott   **DESIGNER** Nicole Ziegler   **CLIENT** Ladder Up

LADDER *up*
FINANCIA

ONE FOR YOU.
www.goladderup.org

ONE TO SHARE.
www.goladderup.org

AMALIA TURKEWITZ
PROGRAM ASSOCIATE
ATURKEWITZ@GOLADDERUP.ORG

233 S WACKER DRIVE, SUITE 9100
CHICAGO IL 60606-6332

T 312.466.0771 : F 312.466.0772

233 S WACKER DRIVE, SUITE 9100
CHICAGO IL 60606-6332

T 312.466.0771
F 312.466.0772

GOLADDERUP.ORG

SA
ON
AS E
AS SHOWIN

THE AVERAGE COST TO HIRE A PAID TAX PREPARER IS $150. LOW
FAMILIES CAN RECEIVE FREE TAX PREPARATION AT TAP. M8:
SMARTER. LEARN HOW TO CLIMB THE ECONOMIC LADDE

cp bing dental surgery ltd

223 Main Road   Tel: +64 4 232 7146
Tawa   Fax: +64 4 232 6611
Wellington 6006   Email: bingdental@paradise.net.nz
New Zealand

bing**dental**

Christopher Bing / Dental Surgeon BDS (Otago)

cp bing dental surgery ltd

223 Main Road   Tel: +64 4 232 7146
Tawa   Fax: +64 4 232 6611
Wellington 6006   Email: bingdental@paradise.net.nz
New Zealand

bing**dental**

Christopher Bing
Dental Surgeon BDS (Otago)

cp bing dental surgery ltd

223 Main Road
Tawa
Wellington 5028
New Zealand
Tel: +64 4 232 7146
Fax: +64 4 232 6611
bingdental@paradise.net

bing**dental**

Christopher Bing
Dental Surgeon BDS (Otago)

cp bing dental surgery ltd

223 Main Road
Tawa
Wellington 6006
New Zealand
Tel: +64 4 232 7146
Fax: +64 4 232 6611
bingdental@paradise.net.nz

bing**dental**

DESIGN FIRM Entermotion Design Studio
DESIGNER Lea Morrow
CLIENT Paste Interacitve

DESIGN FIRM ghost
ART DIRECTOR Matthew Pickett
DESIGNERS Jenkin Hammond
Michael Vidrine
CLIENT ghost

ghost

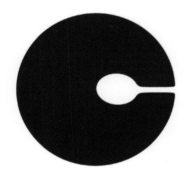

DESIGN FIRM Insight Design Communications
DESIGNER Tracy Holdeman
CLIENT River of Life Worship Center

DESIGN FIRM KAOS advertising
ART DIRECTOR Ian Mavorah
DESIGNER Sarah Rusin
CLIENT Circle Caterers

DESIGN FIRM ghost **ART DIRECTOR** Matthew Pickett **DESIGNERS** Jenkin Hammond, Michael Vidrine **CLIENT** ghost

host

ghost

RNES PRINCIPAL
stadv.com w 405 605 8147 c 405 343 5783 2916A Paseo OKC OK 73103

ghost

ghost

ghost

2916A Paseo OK

ghost

2916A Paseo OKC OK 73103 ghostadv.com

DESIGNER   Keely Jackman
CLIENT   Two Skinny Homos Catering

DESIGN FIRM   Lloyd's Graphic Design Ltd
DESIGNER   Alexander Lloyd
CLIENT   Robinson Forest Management

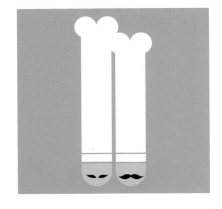

DESIGN FIRM   Masif_Design Affairs
DESIGNER   Carlos Andrés Ortiz G.
CLIENT   Fractal

DESIGN FIRM   Miriello Grafico
ART DIRECTORS   Ron Miriello
Tracy Meiners
DESIGNER   Tracy Meiners
CLIENT   Suturenetics, Inc.

 DESIGN FIRM The Creative Method   **ART DIRECTOR** Tony Ibbotson   **DESIGNER** Mayra Monobe   **CLIENT** The Creative Method

P: +61 (0)2 8231 9977
F: +61 (0)2 8231 9980

STUDIO 10/50 RESERVOIR STREET
SURRY HILLS NSW 2010 AUSTRALIA

E: US@THECREATIVEMETHOD.COM
WWW.THECREATIVEMETHOD.COM

THE
CREATIMETHOD.
STRATEGIC CREATIVE THINKERS

OH THE
POSSIBILITIES

THE
CREATIMETHOD.
STRATEGIC CREATIVE THINKERS

OH THE
POSSIBILITIES

THE
CREATIMETHOD.
STRATEGIC CREATIVE THINKERS

DESIGN FIRM MINE™
ART DIRECTOR Christopher Simmons
DESIGNERS Christopher Simmons
Tim Belonax
CLIENT bil (un)conference

DESIGN FIRM Pavone
ART DIRECTOR Robinson Smith
DESIGNER Gabriel DeNofrio
CLIENT Dauphin County Library System

DESIGN FIRM Rule29 Creative
ART DIRECTOR Justin Ahrens
DESIGNER Kara Ayaram
CLIENT Wonderkind Studios

DESIGNER Sarah Lowe
CLIENT Association for the Study
of the Arts of the Present

DESIGN FIRM Wanja Ledowski STUDIO
DESIGNER Wanja Ledowski
CLIENT miQue

DESIGN FIRM Zync
DESIGNER Marko Zonta
CLIENT Fragile X Research Foundation of Canada

DESIGN FIRM The Infantree
DESIGNER Ryan Smoker
CLIENT Crossway Church

DESIGNER Nicholas Burroughs
CLIENT Central States Petroleum

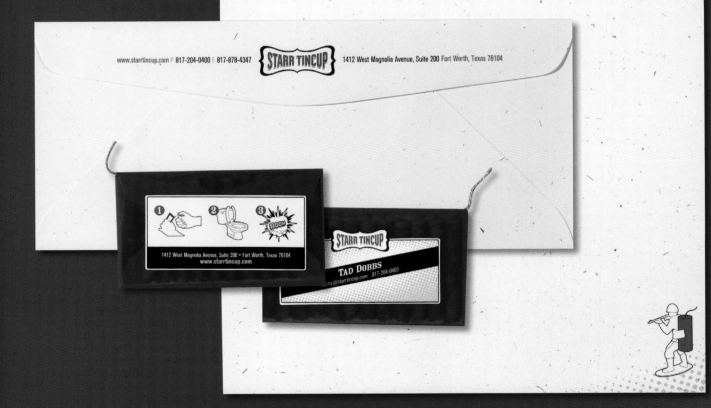

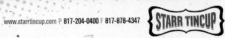

DESIGN FIRM Creative Squall & Starr Tincup **DESIGNER** Tad Dobbs **CLIENT** Starr Tincup

STARR TINCUP

1412 West Magnolia Avenue, Suite 200 Fort Worth, Texas 76104

STARR TINCUP

TAD DOBBS

dobbs@starrtincup.com   817-204-0403

① ② ③ BOOM

1412 West Magnolia Avenue, Suite 200 • Fort Worth, Texas 76104
www.starrtincup.com

DESIGN FIRM Insomniac Design Studio   **DESIGNER** Desiree Walsh Spencer   **CLIENT** Insomniac Design Studio

insomniac design
your brand shouldn't sleep

insomniacdesignstudio

insomniac design
your brand shouldn't sleep

insomniacdesignstudio

CRAFTED

Intentionally inexact and informal

TREEHOUSE
RECORDS

Judges' Selection: Best In Category

This logo artistically fulfills the client's requirement to reflect the casual yet professional nature of their
record label, while intelligently weaving in their desire to have a tree included in the mark.

DESIGN FIRM Juicebox Designs   **DESIGNER** Jay Smith   **ILLUSTRATOR** Kristi Smith   **CLIENT** Treehouse Records

DESIGN FIRM   Alphabet Arm Design
ART DIRECTOR   Aaron Belyea
DESIGNER   Ryan Frease
CLIENT   Flock

DESIGN FIRM   anxious frank design
DESIGNER   Bob Hankin
CLIENT   anxious frank design

THE KENT BELLOWS STUDIO
& Center for Visual Arts

DESIGN FIRM   Capsule
ART DIRECTOR   Brian Adducci
DESIGNER   Michelle Hyster
CLIENT   Milkweed Editions

DESIGN FIRM   Cathy Solarana Design
DESIGNER   Cathy Solarana
CLIENT   The Kent Bellows Studio &
Center for Visual Arts

P.O. Box 24013
Omaha, Neb. 68124
www.coconut-properties.com

(402) 690-4008

STEVE THIESFELD

(402) 690-4008
steve@coconut-properties.com
P.O. Box 24013
www.coconut-properties.com   Omaha, Ne 68124

P.O. Box 24013
Omaha, Neb. 68124
www.coconut-properties.com

BLUEPLANET
NATURAL GRILL

BLUEPLANET
NATURAL GRILL

Dan Tweedy
MANAGER

Blue Planet Natural Grill
6307 Center Street, Suite 101
Omaha, Nebraska 68106

p 402|218-4555   f 866|572-5842
dan@blueplanetnaturalgrill.com

www.blueplanetnaturalgrill.com

6307 Center Street, Suite 101   p 402|218-4555   f 866|572-5842
Omaha, Nebraska 68106   info@blueplanetnaturalgrill.com   www.blueplanetnaturalgrill.com

DESIGN FIRM Cathy Solarana Design   **DESIGNER** Cathy Solarana   **CLIENT** Blue Planet Natural Grill

DESIGNER John Vingoe
CLIENT Rapscallion

DESIGN FIRM Creative Squall
DESIGNER Tad Dobbs
CLIENT Cityview

RADICAL
SKINCARE

DESIGN FIRM Carol McLeod Design
ART DIRECTOR Carol McLeod
DESIGNER Brian Charron
CLIENT Eastland Partners

DESIGN FIRM Damion Hickman Design, Inc.
DESIGNER Damion Hickman
CLIENT Radical Skincare

DESIGN FIRM Damion Hickman Design, Inc.
DESIGNER Damion Hickman
CLIENT Gravity Circle Productions

DESIGN FIRM Entermotion Design Studio
DESIGNER Lea Morrow
CLIENT Yampu Tours & Travel

GRAVITY CIRCLE
PRODUCTIONS

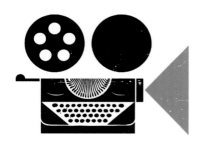

DESIGN FIRM Fuel Inc.
DESIGNERS Bill Bollman
Melissa Gavin
Matt Kempel
Pat Prior
CLIENT Whatsup

DESIGN FIRM J Fletcher Design
DESIGNER Jay Fletcher
CLIENT GreenlitScripts

See where your Rhumb line takes you.
www.rhumbdesigns.com

T 214-573-8711

1900 Elm Street, Suite 506
Dallas, Texas 75201

See where your Rhumb line takes you.

RHUMB
RETAIL DESIGN EXPERTS

Avia Haynes | **Design Manager**

avia@rhumbdesigns.com

T 214-573-8711
C 469-939-9384

1900 Elm Street, Suite 506
Dallas, Texas 75201

www.rhumbdesigns.com

818-19TH AVE SOUTH
NASHVILLE, TN 37203
www.treehouserecords.us

TREEHOUSE
RECORDS

MIKE BETTERTON
VP | GENERAL MANAGER
TEL 615 327 3486

mike@treehouserecords.us

818-19TH AVE SOUTH   NASHVILLE, TN 37203   TEL 615 327 3486   FAX 615 327 3228

DESIGN FIRM Juicebox Designs   DESIGNER Jay Smith   CLIENT Treehouse Records

DESIGN FIRM   Cathy Solarana Design
DESIGNERS   Cathy Solarana
CLIENT   Blue Planet Natural Grill

DESIGN FIRM   KEVIN AKERS dsign + imagery
DESIGNER   Kevin Akers
CLIENT   Bassett Laurel Sweaters

BLUEPLANET
NATURAL GRILL

BASSETT LAUReL

skyleaf

Higglety Pigglety

DESIGN FIRM   Lloyd's Graphic Design Ltd
DESIGNER   Alexander Lloyd
CLIENT   Skyleaf

DESIGN FIRM   Luke Despatie & The Design Firm
DESIGNER   Luke Despatie
CLIENT   Higglety Pigglety

MIDDLE GRADES
PARTNERSHIP

2800 North Charles Street
The Education Building
Baltimore Maryland 21218

tel (410) 516-0175
fax (410) 516-6222

www.middlegradespartnership.org

WHILE YOU LEARN

Sophia L. Rudisill
Associate Director

MIDDLE GRADES
PARTNERSHIP

2800 North Charles Street
The Education Building
Baltimore Maryland 21218

email srudisil1@jhu.edu

office (410) 516-6113
fax (410) 516-6222

www.middlegradespartnership.org

MIDDLE GRADES
PARTNERSHIP

2800 North Charles Street
The Education Building
Baltimore Maryland 21218

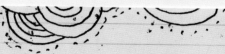

MISSION

The Middle Grades Partnership supports partnerships between public and independent schools to provide comprehensive summer and after-school learning opportunities for academically promising Baltimore City middle school students so that they may thrive in rigorous high schools, college and beyond. Through this work, the Middle Grades Partnership aspires to provide a core of leadership for Baltimore.

DESIGN FIRM   Mad Dog Graphx
DESIGNER   Kris Ryan-Clarke
CLIENT   Core Pilates

DESIGN FIRM   Ramp Creative + Design
DESIGNER   Michael Stinson
CLIENT   Denimhead

DESIGN FIRM   Rule29 Creative
ART DIRECTOR   Justin Ahrens
DESIGNERS   Justin Ahrens
Kerri Liu
CLIENT   Life In Abundance

DESIGN FIRM   Shari Margolin Design
DESIGNER   Shari Margolin
CLIENT   The Little Wine Shop

forty four / 44 steep hill / lincoln LN2 1LU
01522 527516 / www.fortyfourshop.co.uk /
fortyfoursteephill@btinternet.com

hope to see you soon!

forty four / 44 steep hill / lincoln LN2 1LU
01522 527516 / www.fortyfourshop.co.uk /
fortyfoursteephill@btinternet.com

DESIGN FIRM Stitch Design Co. **DESIGNER** Courtney Rowson **CLIENT** Gayle Brooker Photography

DESIGN FIRM Stitch Design Co.
DESIGNERS Courtney Rowson
Amy Pastre
CLIENT Shadow Lane Farms

DESIGN FIRM Tom Varisco Designs
ART DIRECTOR Tom Varisco
DESIGNERS Tom Varisco
Loren Stephens
Gregory Good
CLIENT Newcomb College and
New Orleans Museum of Art

DESIGN FIRM What Cheer, Inc.
DESIGNER John Henry Müller
CLIENT MindMixer

DESIGN FIRM RDQLUS Creative
DESIGNER Steve Gordon Jr
CLIENT Expeditiously Delicious

DIMENSIONAL

Realistic and playful use of light and shadow

Judges' Selection: Best In Category

In this logo inspired by the salon's name, the sophisticated play between
a hair brush and a paintbrush artfully describes the client's business.

DESIGN FIRM Stitch Design Co.   **DESIGNERS** Amy Pastre, Courtney Rowson   **CLIENT** Canvas Hair Salon

DESIGN FIRM Agent OX
DESIGNER Sarah Osborn
CLIENT Agent OX

DESIGN FIRM Alphabet Arm Design
ART DIRECTOR Aaron Belyea
DESIGNER Chris Piascik
CLIENT Second Glass

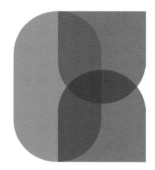

DESIGN FIRM Creative Media
DESIGNER Nigel Morrison
CLIENT Health Promoting College /
Southern Regional College

DESIGN FIRM Design Nut
ART DIRECTORS Alan Feldenkris
Brent Almond
DESIGNERS Brent Almond
Sharisse Steber
CLIENT The Nature Conservancy

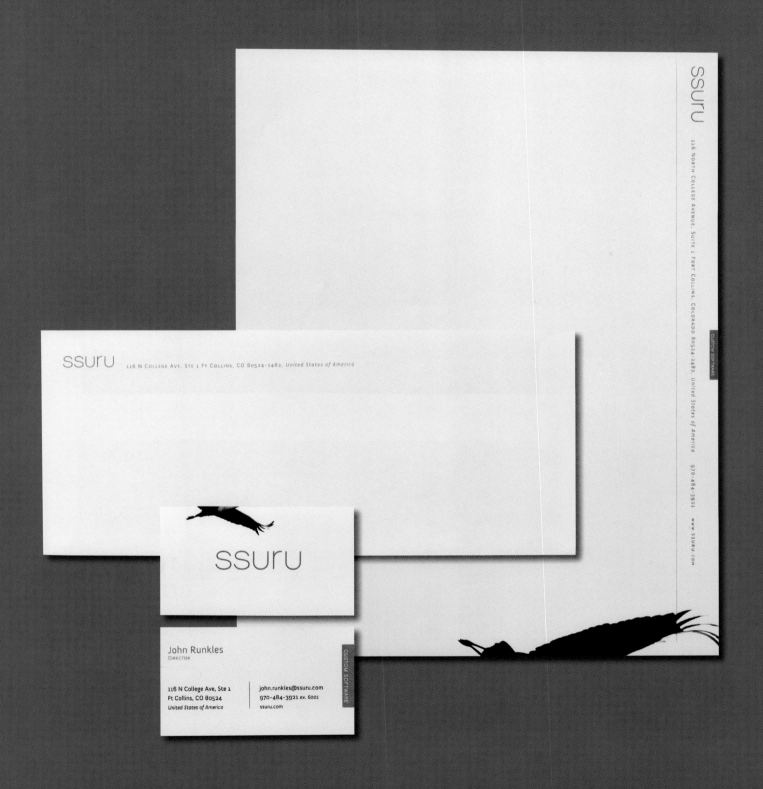

BARLOW & BISHOP
AMERICA EUROPE RUSSIA

BARLOW & BISHOP
AMERICA EUROPE RUSSIA

BARLOW & BISHOP
AMERICA EUROPE RUSSIA

BB
AMERICA EUROPE RUSSIA

KAROLINE KABLE
SENIOR DESIGNER

11 PRINCESS STREET, CHARLESTON, SC 29401
843 277 2775 /TEL 843 278 9324 /FAX
KAROLINE@BARLOWANDBISHOP.COM

WWW.BARLOWANDBISHOP.COM

DESIGN FIRM Stitch Design Co.   **DESIGNERS** Amy Pastre, Courtney Rowson   **CLIENT** Barlow & Bishop

BARLOW & BISHOP
AMERICA EUROPE RUSSIA

BARLOW & BIS
AMERICA EUROPE RUSSIA

KAROLINE KABLE
SENIOR DESIGNER
11 PRINCESS STREET, CHARLESTON, SC 29401
843 277 2775 /TEL   843 278 9324 /FAX
KAROLINE@BARLOWANDBISHOP.COM
WWW.BARLOWANDBISHOP.COM

DESIGN FIRM   Fixation Marketing
DESIGNER   Brent Almond
CLIENT   A2Z

DESIGN FIRM   HOOK
DESIGNER   Brady Waggoner
CLIENT   Lowcountry Boil

DESIGN FIRM   Lloyd's Graphic Design Ltd
DESIGNER   Alexander Lloyd
CLIENT   McCarthy Law

DESIGN FIRM   Lloyd's Graphic Design Ltd
DESIGNER   Alexander Lloyd
CLIENT   Aquaculture Direct

Send 1819 Colorado Avenue, Santa Monica, CA 90404
Call 310.401.2220 Visit newhat.tv

90404 Call 310.401.2220 Visit newhat.com

NEW
HAT

NEW
HAT

NEW
HAT

DESIGN FIRM Ramp Creative + Design   DESIGNER Michael Stinson   CLIENT New Hat

DESIGN FIRM   Miriello Grafico
ART DIRECTORS   Ron Miriello
                Tracy Meiners
DESIGNER   Tracy Meiners
CLIENT   Smarter Foods

DESIGN FIRM   Rhythm Behavior
DESIGNER   Natasha Kramskaya
CLIENT   Mankutek

DESIGN FIRM   Stebbings Partners
CLIENT   Media Lantern

DESIGN FIRM   Stebbings Partners
CLIENT   Children's Hospital Boston

DESIGN FIRM   Stebbings Partners
CLIENT   Stebbings Partners

DESIGN FIRM   Studio928
DESIGNER   Chris Braun
CLIENT   Ambiance

DESIGN FIRM   Studio Cream Design
DESIGNER   John Valastro
CLIENT   Cycling Central:
SBS Television, Australia

DESIGN FIRM   Studio Cream Design
DESIGNER   John Valastro
CLIENT   CP (Computer Professionals) :
Australian Computer Society

T 704 519.7163
F 866 405.5932

7046 ROCKY FALLS RD
CHARLOTTE, NC 28211

www.BELLMAS.com

ARMANDO BELLMAS

armando@bellmas.com

T 704 519.7163
F 866 405.5932

7046 ROCKY FALLS RD
CHARLOTTE, NC 28211

www.BELLMAS.com

ARMANDO BELLMAS

armando@bellmas.com

DEBBIE BEATTIE
Communications Director

OAK HEIGHTS ESTATE WINERY
337 Covert Hill Road, RR #1
Warkworth, Ontario K0K 3K0

email debbie@oakheights.ca
mobile 905.269.1769
phone 705.924.9625
toll free 1.866.625.6051

www.oakheights.ca

DESIGN FIRM Luke Despatie & The Design Firm   DESIGNER Luke Despatie   CLIENT Oak Heights

DESIGN FIRM Wing Chan Design, Inc.
ART DIRECTOR Wing Chan
DESIGNER Onny Jap
CLIENT synexis cg

DESIGN FIRM Wonderwheel Creative
DESIGNER Tim Merrill
CLIENT Wonderwheel Creative

DESIGN FIRM 3rd Edge
ART DIRECTOR Frankie Gonzalez
DESIGNER Nick Schmitz
CLIENT Grupo Recurso

DESIGN FIRM 5Seven
ART DIRECTORS Phoebe Smith
Scott Spector
Clint Delapaz
DESIGNER Clint Delapaz
CLIENT Pensare Group

FEMININE

Softness and subtlety via curves and color

REGAL

Literary

Judges' Selection: Best In Category

Regal Literary is a representation agency with a tradition of cultivating its authors' talents and careers. The hummingbird perfectly conveys the energy, curious spirit, and off-beat sensibilities the client wants to capture in their logo.

DESIGN FIRM The O Group   **ART DIRECTORS** Jason B. Cohen, J. Kenneth Rothermich   **DESIGNER** J. Kenneth Rothermich   **CLIENT** Regal Literary

DESIGN FIRM   Amy Lewis Design
ART DIRECTOR   Amy Lewis
DESIGN   Lindsay Gardiner
CLIENT   Silver Spoon Estate

DESIGN FIRM   Archrival
DESIGNER   Joel Kreutzer
CLIENT   Nomad Lounge

DESIGN FIRM   Cathy Solarana Design
DESIGNER   Cathy Solarana
CLIENT   Moseley Photography

DESIGN FIRM   Cathy Solarana Design
ART DIRECTORS Cathy Solarana
               Dave Markes
DESIGNER   Cathy Solarana
CLIENT   Cathy Solarana Design

James Bednarski
james@choosesurroundings.com

c 317.590.3039
t 317.575.0482
f 317.575.9818
choosesurroundings.com

421 South Rangeline Rd.
Carmel, IN 46032

SURROUNDINGS
BY NATUREWORKS+

SURROUNDINGS
BY NATUREWORKS+
421 South Rangeline Rd, Carmel, IN 46032

t 317.575.0482
f 317.575.9818
choosesurroundings.com

421 South Rangeline Rd.
Carmel, IN 46032

DESIGN FIRM Stitch Design Co. **DESIGNER** Courtney Rowson **CLIENT** Blue Moon Events

AMSER TE
WWW.AMSERTE.CO.UK

AMSER TE
WWW.AMSERTE.CO.UK

AMSER TE
WWW.AMSERTE.CO.UK

HURIO LLESTRI A
NWYDDAU FINTAGE

VINTAGE CROCKERY &
ACCESSORIES HIRE

BETHAN THOMAS

6 KING STREET
PENARTH
BRO MORGANNWG
VALE OF GLAMORGAN
CF64 1HQ

029 2070 9527
BETHAN@AMSERTE.CO.UK
078 5528 2805

AMSER TE, 6 KING STREET, PENARTH, BRO MORGANNWG, VALE OF GLAMORGAN, CF64 1HQ
FF/T: 029 2070 9527 / 078 552 828 05   E: BETHAN@AMSERTE.CO.UK   WWW.AMSERTE.CO.UK

AMSER TE, 6 KING STREET, PENARTH, BRO MORGANNWG, VALE OF GLAMORGAN, CF64 1HQ
FF/T: 029 2070 9527 / 078 552 828 05   E: BETHAN@AMSERTE.CO.UK
WWW.AMSERTE.CO.UK

DESIGN FIRM Kutchibok   **ART DIRECTOR** Siôn Dafydd   **DESIGNER** Alwyn Thomas   **CLIENT** Amser Te

DESIGN FIRM   CINDERBLOC
DESIGNERS   Ryan Di Leo
   Michael Nitsopoulos
CLIENT   eka

DESIGN FIRM   CINDERBLOC
DESIGNERS   Ryan Di Leo
   Michael Nitsopoulos
CLIENT   Boobyball

DESIGN FIRM   DogStar
DESIGNER   Rodney Davidson
CLIENT   Ann Bell Alford

DESIGN FIRM   EAT Advertising and Design
ART DIRECTOR   Patrice Jobe
DESIGNERS   Rachel Eilts
   DeAnne Dodd
CLIENT   Contour MD

801 673 4676
MOBILE

801 295 3420
FACSIMILE

PHILIMINA
SPACE   LIGHT   COLOR
HARMONY

PHILIMINA
HARMONY

JEFF OLSEN
EXECUTIVE VICE PRESIDENT
JEFF@PHILIMINA.COM   FX 801-295-3420
801 243 5959

PHILIMINA
1977 SOUTH 800 EAST   BOUNTIFUL UTAH
84010

PHILIMINA.COM
1977 SOUTH 800 EAST   BOUNTIFUL UTAH 84010

DESIGN FIRM Rare Method, Salt Lake   ART DIRECTOR Jeff Olsen   DESIGNERS Brian McDonough, Tonya Olsen   CLIENT Philimina Interiors

PHILIMINA

HARMONY

DESIGN FIRM   GoodTwin Design, Inc.
DESIGNER   Adam Nielsen
CLIENT   Orchid Foundry

DESIGN FIRM   J Fletcher Design
DESIGNER   Jay Fletcher
CLIENT   Charleston Naturally

DESIGN FIRM   Kanella
DESIGNER   Kanella Arapoglou
CLIENT   Dr. Yiannis Vamvakaris

DESIGN FIRM   KEVIN AKERS design + imagery
DESIGNER   Kevin Akers
CLIENT   Bella Pictures

DESIGN FIRM Lloyd's Graphic Design Ltd
DESIGNER Alexander Lloyd
CLIENT The Secret Garden

DESIGN FIRM Luke Despatie & The Design Firm
DESIGNER Luke Despatie
CLIENT Toronto Body Works

The Secret Garden

toronto bodyworks

DESIGN FIRM Melissa Wehrman Design
DESIGNER Melissa Wehrman
CLIENT Zwilling Needlepoint Designs

DESIGN FIRM One Man's Studio
DESIGNER Keith Kitz
CLIENT Hue Amour

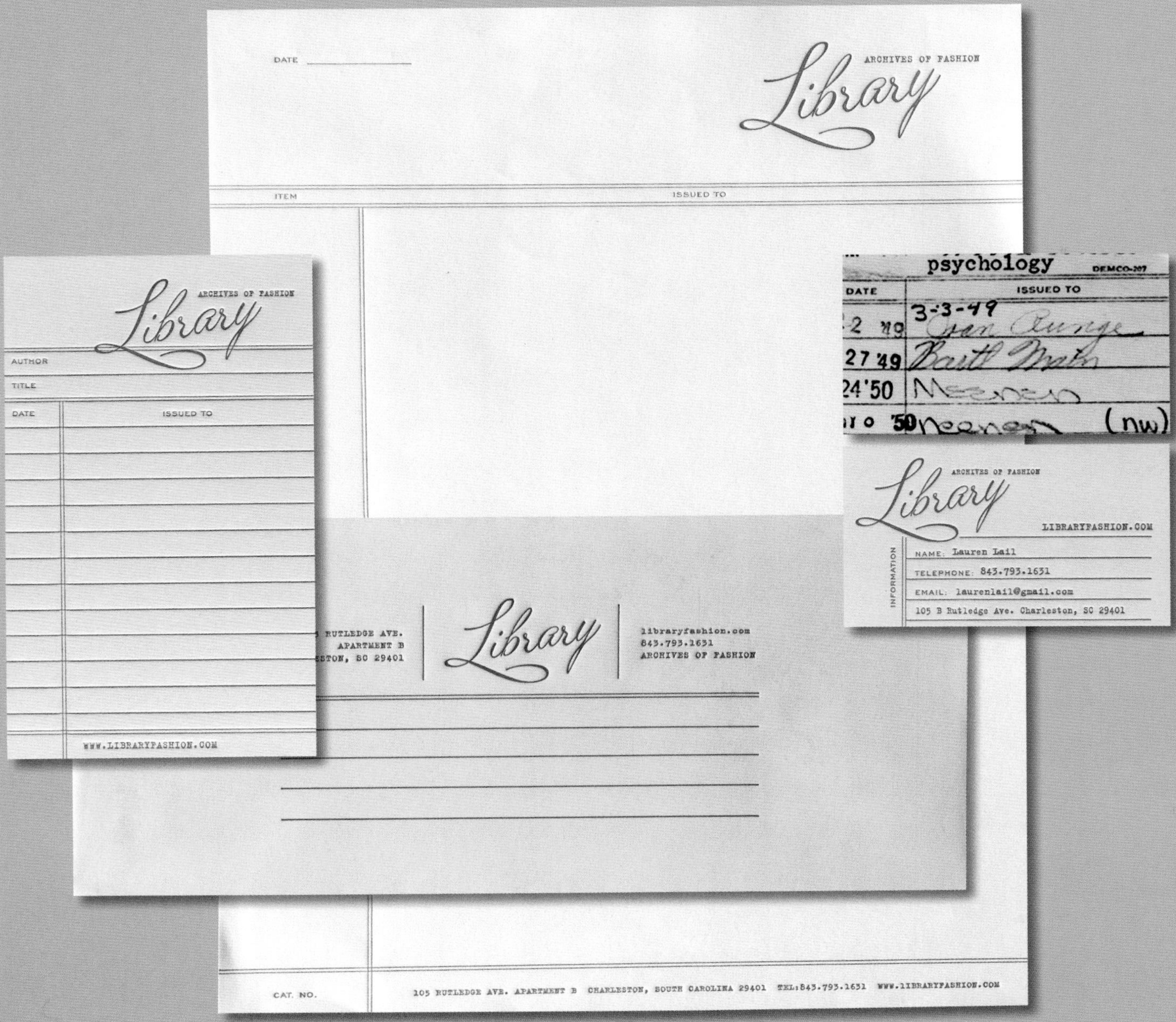

DESIGN FIRM Stitch Design Co.   **DESIGNER** Courtney Rowson   **CLIENT** Library: Archives of Fashion

ARCHIVES OF FASHION

Library

LIB

INFORMATION

NAME: Lauren Lail

TELEPHONE: 843.793.1631

EMAIL: laurenlail@gmail.com

105 B Rutledge Ave. Charleston, S

ARCHIVES OF FASHION

Library

ISSUED TO

AUTHOR

TITLE

DATE

ISSUED TO

DESIGN FIRM CINDERBLOC **DESIGNERS** Ryan Di Leo, Michael Nitsopoulos **CLIENT** Bellvue Manor

b

BELLVUE
MANOR

...MANOR·COM

...t Vaughan Ontario L4K 2M7
...761 7988

8081 Jane Street Vaughan Ontario L4K 2M7
{ T | F } 905 761 7288 905 761 7988

...·COM

DESIGN FIRM   The Pink Orange
DESIGNER   Rebecca Ashby
CLIENT   Binx

DESIGN FIRM   Rule29 Creative
ART DIRECTOR   Justin Ahrens
DESIGNER   Kara Ayaram
CLIENT   Davidson Designs

DESIGN FIRM   Stebbings Partners
CLIENT   Muchos

DESIGN FIRM   Pluck™ The Division of Graphic
Perception & Design Research
DESIGNER   Seth Levy
CLIENT   Sevy Creative

DESIGN FIRM Stitch Design Co.
DESIGNERS Courtney Rowson
Amy Pastre
CLIENT Pearl Lexington

DESIGN FIRM Studio Cream Design
DESIGNER John Valastro
CLIENT Inika Pty Ltd

INIKA

DESIGN FIRM Up Inc.
ART DIRECTOR Carey George
DESIGNER Van Chong
CLIENT Fairmont Hotels & Resorts

DESIGN FIRM WORKtoDATE
DESIGNER Greg Bennett
CLIENT theCOUNTERcorps

DESIGN FIRM Stitch Design Co.   **DESIGNERS** Amy Pastre, Courtney Rowson   **CLIENT** Tara Guérard Soirée

ILLUSTRATED

Visually intricate but conceptually clear

Judges' Selection: Best In Category

This logo was selected because the perfectly-rendered, seamless combination
of a soccer ball and a ladybug makes it ideal for the local girls' soccer team.

DESIGN FIRM Flight Deck Creative   **DESIGNER** Jason Rahn   **CLIENT** Lady Bugs Soccer Team

DESIGN FIRM   Archrival
ART DIRECTOR   Clint! Runge
DESIGNER   Joel Kreutzer
CLIENT   Smooth Ambler Spirits

DESIGN FIRM   Alphabet Arm Design
ART DIRECTOR   Aaron Belyea
DESIGNER   Ryan Frease
CLIENT   Music Van Productions

DESIGN FIRM   DogStar
DESIGNER   Rodney Davidson
CLIENT   Mark Gooch

DESIGN FIRM   Design Trust
ART DIRECTORS   Dan Schuster
Sarah Ordover
DESIGNER   Dan Schuster
CLIENT   NewBo City Market

Connecting your brand with your essence.

Connecting your brand with your essence.

DESIGN FIRM Sussner Design Company   **ART DIRECTOR** Derek Sussner   **DESIGNER** Brandon Van Liere   **CLIENT** Reflections

Peace of mind is our
SATISFACTION GUARANTEE

MAILING ADDRESS
2229 EDGEWOOD AVE. S
MINNEAPOLIS, MN 55426

TEL 952 925 5100
FAX 952 925 5111

RESPONSIVE
RESOURCEFUL
RESULTS
REFLECTIONS-PRT.C

CHRIS CLEMENS PRESIDENT
EML CJC@PRINTBETTER.COM

 DESIGN FIRM Miles Design **DESIGNER** Brian K Gray **CLIENT** BRAND PHOTODESIGN

DESIGN FIRM   Diseño Dos Asociados
ART DIRECTORS Juan Carlos García
               Carlos Rivera
DESIGNER   Víctor Martínez
CLIENT   Vegetalistos

DESIGN FIRM   Diseño Dos Asociados
ART DIRECTORS Juan Carlos García
               Carlos Rivera
DESIGNERS   Mariana Jiménez
               Juan Carlos García
CLIENT   Chile Ajo

DESIGN FIRM   Extra Crispy Creative
DESIGNER   Paul Mitchell
CLIENT   White Label Vineyard

DESIGN FIRM   Flight Deck Creative
DESIGNER   Jason Rahn
CLIENT   Flight Deck Creative

DESIGN FIRM   Insight Design Communications
DESIGNER   Tracy Holdeman
CLIENT   Colorado Premium:
Trailhead Brand Meats

DESIGN FIRM   Insight Design Communications
DESIGNER   Tracy Holdeman
CLIENT   Lost Art Development Co.

DESIGN FIRM   Insight Design Communications
DESIGNER   Tracy Holdeman
CLIENT   Colorado Premium:
5280 Brand Meats - Top Quality Premium

DESIGN FIRM   Insight Design Communications
DESIGNER   Tracy Holdeman
CLIENT   Colorado Premium:
Prospector Brand Meats – Economy Meats

DESIGN FIRM Insight Design Communications
DESIGNER Tracy Holdeman
CLIENT Holzer Marketing

DESIGN FIRM J. Sayles Design Co.
ART DIRECTOR John Sayles
DESIGNERS John Sayles
Doug Zimmerman
CLIENT Marion County Fair

DESIGN FIRM Jeremy Slagle Graphic Design
DESIGNER Jeremy Slagle
CLIENT Seagull Bags

DESIGN FIRM Kindred Design Studio
DESIGNER Steve Redmond
CLIENT Graze

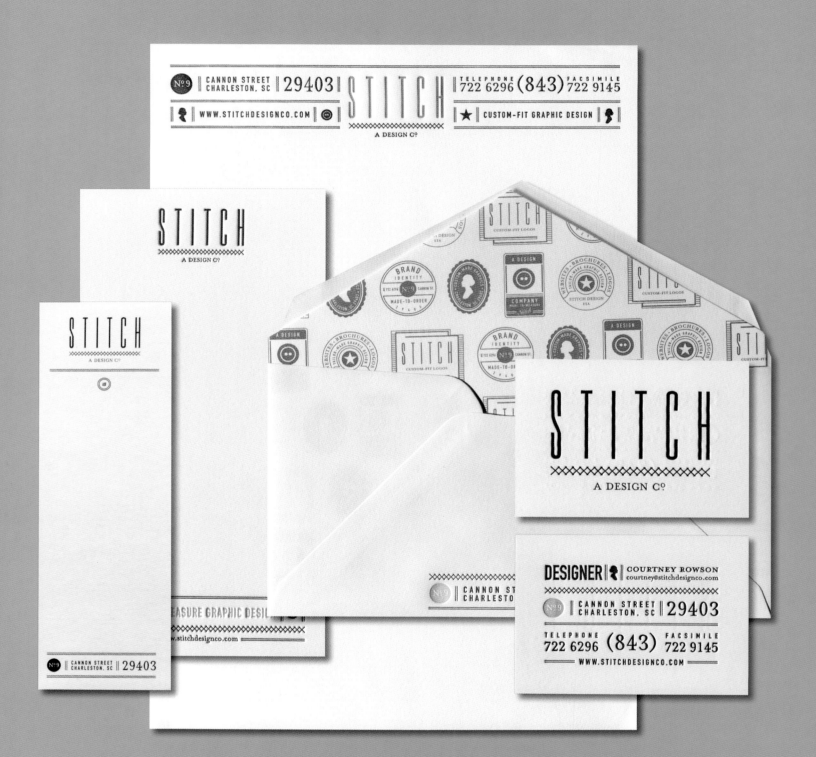

DESIGN FIRM Stitch Design Co. **DESIGNERS** Amy Pastre, Courtney Rowson **CLIENT** Stitch Design Co.

DESIGN FIRM   Red Eye Graphic Design
DESIGNER   Mitch Johnson
CLIENT   Ogallala High School Athletics

DESIGN FIRM   Red Eye Graphic Design
DESIGNER   Mitch Johnson
CLIENT   Dubuque Hockey Club

EST⁽ᴰ⁾ 1978

LEADERSHIP
FOUNDATIONS

Latitudes

DESIGN FIRM   Sussner Design Company
ART DIRECTOR   Derek Sussner
DESIGNER   Brandon Van Liere
CLIENT   Leadership Foundations

DESIGN FIRM   3 Advertising
ART DIRECTOR   Sam Maclay
DESIGNER   Jesse Arneson
CLIENT   Latitudes

LINEAR

Linework that balances simplicity and charm

Judges' Selection: Best In Category

Llerandi is a holding company focused in the robotics and construction industries.
This rendering of a robotic horse is the perfect metaphor for the company's strength and power.

DESIGN FIRM Diseño Dos Asociados   **ART DIRECTORS** Juan Carlos García, Carlos Rivera   **DESIGNER** Víctor Martínez   **CLIENT** Llerandi

DESIGNER   Alexander Wende
CLIENT   ROAST Coffee and Espresso Bars

DESIGN FIRM   Capsule
ART DIRECTOR   Brian Adducci
DESIGNERS   Brian Adducci
Greg Brose
CLIENT   StoneRiver

ROAST™
COFFEE & ESPRESSO BARS

STONERIVER™

artissimo
bakehouse

mamakita®

DESIGN FIRM   Chris Trivizas | Design
ART DIRECTOR   Chris Trivizas
DESIGNERS   Chris Trivizas
George Strouzas
CLIENT   Artissimo LTD

DESIGN FIRM   Chris Trivizas | Design
ART DIRECTOR   Chris Trivizas
DESIGNERS   Chris Trivizas
George Strouzas
CLIENT   Mamakita

Angelique J. Miller
interior designer // NCIDQ certified
amiller@tonoarchitects.com

T 717
735
8166

717
735
TONOARCHITECTS.COM   F 8169

T 717
735
8166

717
735
D. Hunter Johnson   F 8169
principal architect // AIA, NCARB   114 E CHESTNUT ST // LANCASTER, PA 17602

DESIGN FIRM PARAGON Marketing Communications **DESIGNER** Louai Alasfahani **CLIENT** PARAGON Marketing Communications

PARAGON
MARKETING COMMUNICATIONS

DESIGN FIRM TOKY Branding + Design **ART DIRECTORS** Eric Thoelke, Katy Fischer **DESIGNER** Mary Rosamond **CLIENT** David Richard Contemporary

DESIGN FIRM   Creative Squall
DESIGNER   Tad Dobbs
CLIENT   Creative Squall

DESIGN FIRM   DogStar
DESIGNER   Rodney Davidson
CLIENT   Provenance Digital

CREATIVE
SQUALL

PROVENANCE

brand·in·chef

DESIGN FIRM   Diseño Dos Asociados
ART DIRECTORS   Juan Carlos García
Carlos Rivera
DESIGNER   Juan Carlos García
CLIENT   Brand in Chef

DESIGN FIRM   EIGA Design
ART DIRECTORS   Elisabeth Plass
Henning Otto
DESIGNER   Nicola Janssen
CLIENT   Stiftung Deutsch-Russischer
Jugendaustausch

Linear

113

DESIGN FIRM FreshBrand
DESIGNER Marcel Venter
CLIENT Consilium

DESIGN FIRM Geyrhalter & Company
ART DIRECTOR Fabian Geyrhalter
DESIGNER Kari Yu
CLIENT Mindshare

Consilium

Mindshare
Los Angeles

Nature's
kitchen™

DESIGN FIRM J Fletcher Design
DESIGNER Jay Fletcher
CLIENT Charleston Peace One Day

DESIGN FIRM Janus:
DESIGNER Aleksandar Petrovic
CLIENT Nation's Kitchen

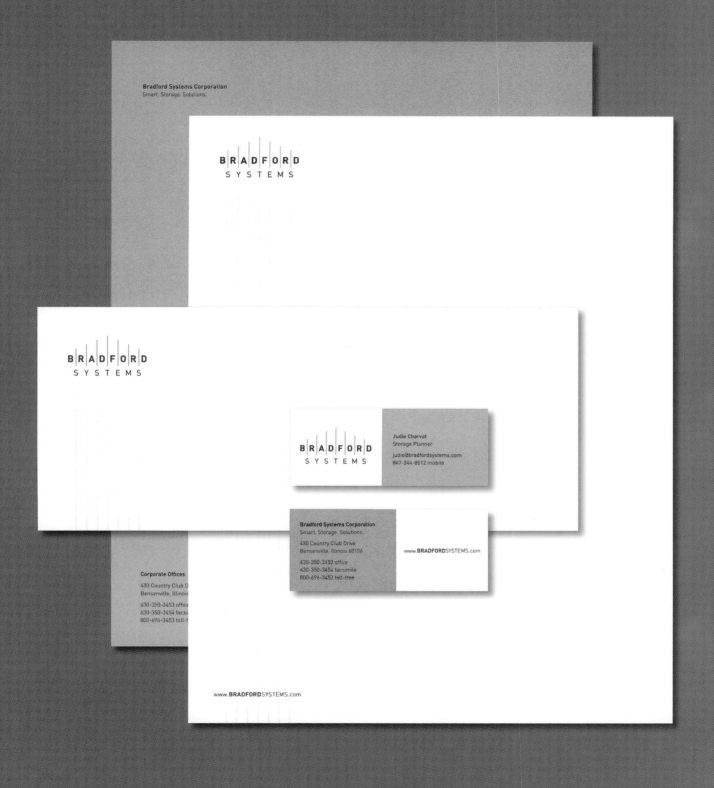

Bradford Systems Corporation
Smart. Storage. Solutions.

B R A D F O R D
S Y S T E M S

B R A D F O R D
S Y S T E M S

Judie Charvat
Storage Planner

judie@bradfordsystems.com
847-344-8512 mobile

Bradford Systems Corporation
Smart. Storage. Solutions.

430 Country Club Drive
Bensenville, Illinois 60106

630-350-3453 office
630-350-3454 facsimile
800-696-3453 toll-free

www.**BRADFORD**SYSTEMS.com

Corporate Offices

430 Country Club D
Bensenville, Illinois

630-350-3453 office
630-350-3454 facsi
800-696-3453 toll-f

www.**BRADFORD**SYSTEMS.com

ydesign

ydesign **David Yugovich
Creative Director**
3763 North High Street, Suite C
Columbus, Ohio 43214
614.559.3956
dyugovich@ydesigncreative.com
www.ydesigncreative.com

3763 North High Street, Suite C, Columbus, Ohio 43214
614.559.3956 www.ydesigncreative.com

DESIGN FIRM Jeremy Slagle Graphic Design **DESIGNER** Jeremy Slagle **CLIENT** ydesign

ydesign

David Yugovich
Creative Director
3753 North High Street, Suite C
Columbus, Ohio 43214
614.859.2055
dyugovich@ydesigncreative.c...
www.ydesigncreative.com

DESIGN FIRM Mirko Ilić Corp. **ART DIRECTOR** Mirko Ilić **DESIGNER** Jee-eun Lee, Mirko Ilić **CLIENT** Patina Restaurant Group

DESIGN FIRM MINE™
ART DIRECTOR Christopher Simmons
DESIGNERS Christopher Simmons
Tim Belonax
CLIENT California Film Institute

DESIGN FIRM MINE™
ART DIRECTOR Christopher Simmons
DESIGNERS Christopher Simmons
Tim Belonax
CLIENT Scheyer SF

MILL VALLEY
FILM FESTIVAL

DESIGN FIRM Niedermeier Design
DESIGNER Kurt Niedermeier
CLIENT Teluu

DESIGN FIRM Niedermeier Design
DESIGNER Kurt Niedermeier
CLIENT Netrunner

DESIGN FIRM   Janus
DESIGNER   Aleksandar Petrovic
CLIENT   Serbian Railways

DESIGN FIRM   Jarheadesign
DESIGNER   Jarred Katz
CLIENT   Kroehler Coastal Home

ŽELEZNICE SRBIJE

KROEHLER
COASTAL HOME

PATHOS

DESIGN FIRM   Kanella
DESIGNER   Kanella Arapoglou
CLIENT   Mihalopoulos Ltd.

DESIGN FIRM   KEVIN AKERS design + imagery
DESIGNER   Kevin Akers
CLIENT   C-Gull Inc.

DESIGN FIRM   Niedermeier Design
DESIGNER   Kurt Niedermeier
CLIENT   CloudSwitch

DESIGN FIRM   onetreeink
DESIGNER   Marcos Calamato
CLIENT   Adora

DESIGN FIRM   Owen Jones Design
DESIGNER   Owen Jones
CLIENT   Pieces&Bits

DESIGN FIRM   p11creative
ART DIRECTOR   Lance Huante
DESIGNER   Ty Mattson
CLIENT   Sares•Regis Group

DESIGN FIRM A3 Design **ART DIRECTOR** Amanda Altman **DESIGNER** Alan Altman, Rachel Giralico **CLIENT** A3 Design

DESIGN FIRM Pluck™ The Division of Graphic
Perception & Design Research
DESIGNER Seth Levy
CLIENT Genuine First Aid

DESIGN FIRM Stebbings Partners
CLIENT Bucu

READY FOR REFORM

DESIGN FIRM Tiffany M. Chen Design
DESIGNER Tiffany Chen
CLIENT Bidcation, LLC

DESIGNER Ian Ingalls
CLIENT Ready For Reform

MASCULINE

Power, mass, and distinction

Judges' Selection: Best In Category

The challenge presented by this client was to make a logo that leveraged the power of the name RIOT without negative connotations. Since megaphones can be used by both sides of a riot, it's a flawless metaphor.

DESIGN FIRM HOOK   **DESIGNERS** Brady Waggoner   **CLIENT** RIOT Outfitters

DESIGN FIRM ATOMICvibe
DESIGNER Jon Stapp
CLIENT The Cleaning Corps

DESIGN FIRM CINDERBLOC
DESIGNERS Ryan Di Leo
Michael Nitsopoulos
CLIENT NEWMAN

DESIGN FIRM EXPLORARE
ART DIRECTORS Juan Carlos Henaine
Paola Aja
DESIGNER Omar Salinas
CLIENT VissorPav

DESIGN FIRM Fuel
DESIGNERS Bill Bollman
Melissa Gavin
Matt Kempel
Lance Lethcoe
Pat Prior
CLIENT Bachman

KING BEAN

COFFEE ROASTERS
CHARLESTON, SOUTH CAROLINA

PHONE 843 722 7650   SINCE 1984   FAX 843 744 8652

3356 MEETING ST. RD.   N. CHARLESTON, SC 29405

KING BEAN COFFEE ROASTERS
WWW.KINGBEAN.COM

KURT WEINBERGER

3356 MEETING ST. RD.   N. CHARLESTON, SC 29405

KING BEAN COFFEE ROASTERS
WWW.KINGBEAN.COM

KING BEAN

COFFEE ROASTERS
CHARLESTON, SOUTH CAROLINA

DESIGN FIRM Stitch Design Co.   **DESIGNERS** Amy Pastre, Courtney Rowson   **CLIENT** King Bean Coffee

TROUBADOUR

TROUBADOUR
478 KING STREET, SUITE 2
CHARLESTON, SOUTH CAROLINA
29403

TROUBADOUR

TROUBADOUR

TROUBADOUR
LINDSEY CARTER

910.431.3024   LINDSEY@TROUBADOURCLOTHING.COM
WWW.TROUBADOURCLOTHING.COM

DESIGN FIRM Stitch Design Co.   DESIGNERS Amy Pastre, Courtney Rowson   CLIENT Troubadour Clothing

DESIGN FIRM GoodTwin Design, Inc.
ART DIRECTOR Adam Nielsen
DESIGNER Joshua Schwieger
CLIENT StickerMan

DESIGN FIRM Insight Design Communications
DESIGNER Tracy Holdeman
CLIENT Catalyst Marketing

DESIGN FIRM Insight Design Communications
DESIGNER Tracy Holdeman
CLIENT Carlos O'Kelly's Mexican Café:
Golf Tournament Logo

DESIGN FIRM Jeremy Slagle Graphic Design
DESIGNER Jeremy Slagle
CLIENT Dennis Automotive

DESIGN FIRM   Rule29 Creative
ART DIRECTOR   Justin Ahrens
DESIGNER   Tim Damitz
CLIENT   Team Red White & Blue

DESIGN FIRM   Stebbings Partners
CLIENT   City Diner

DESIGN FIRM   Stitch Design Co.
DESIGNERS   Courtney Rowson
     Amy Pastre
CLIENT   King Bean Coffee

DESIGN FIRM   Tenfold Collective
ART DIRECTOR   Josh Emrich
DESIGNER   Sara Seal
CLIENT   Grimm Brothers Brewhouse

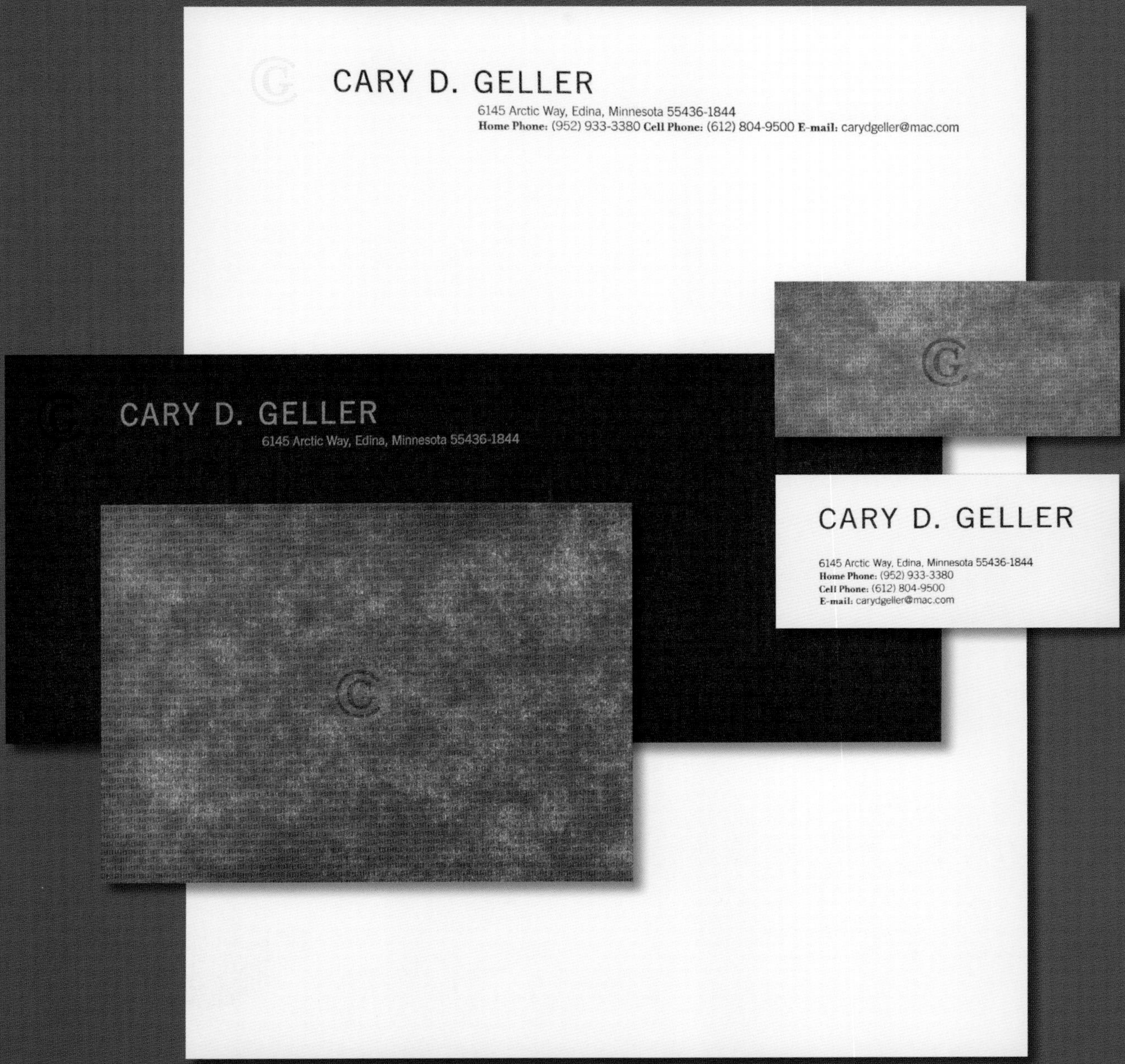

DESIGN FIRM Sussner Design Company **ART DIRECTOR** Derek Sussner **DESIGNER** Jamie Paul **CLIENT** Cary Geller

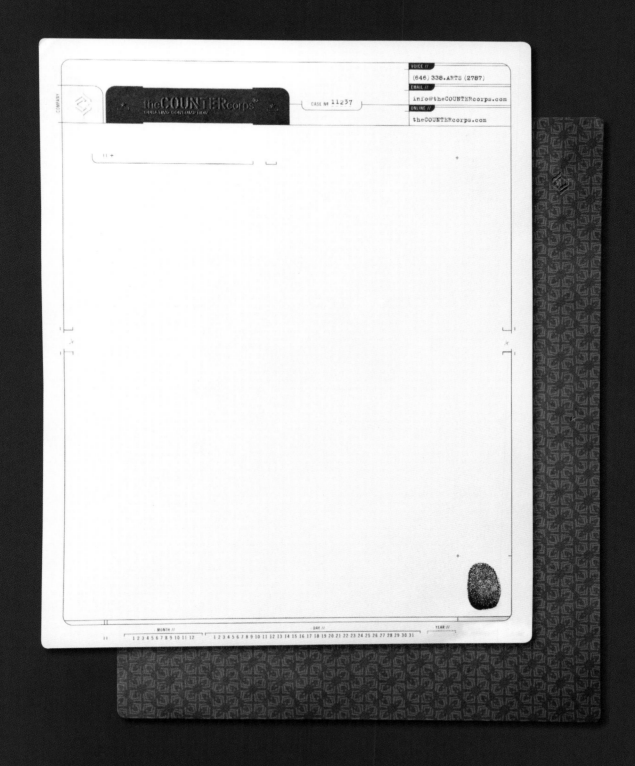

DESIGN FIRM WORKtoDATE   **DESIGNER** Greg Bennett   **CLIENT** theCOUNTERcorps

DESIGN FIRM Tenfold Collective
ART DIRECTOR Christopher McLaughlin
DESIGNER Josh Emrich
CLIENT Novo Restoration, Inc.

DESIGN FIRM Tenfold Collective
ART DIRECTOR Josh Emrich
DESIGNER Sara Seal
CLIENT Feynman School

DESIGN FIRM TOKY Branding + Design
ART DIRECTOR Eric Thoelke
DESIGNER Travis Brown
CLIENT Midtown Alley

DESIGN FIRM TOKY Branding + Design
ART DIRECTOR Eric Thoelke
DESIGNER Travis Brown
CLIENT Stadium Grill

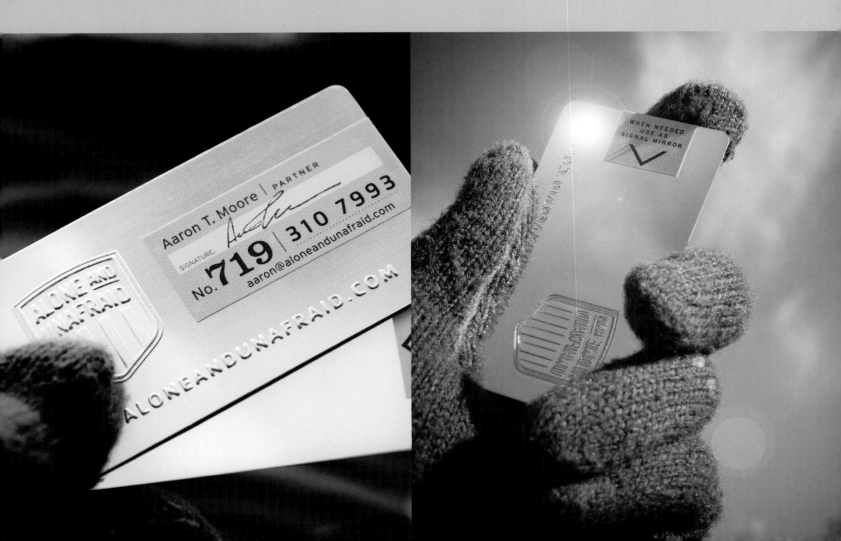

DESIGN FIRM 3 Advertising **ART DIRECTOR** Sam Maclay **DESIGNER** Tim McGrath **CLIENT** Scott Boswell Enterprises

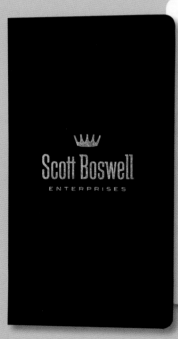

Stella!

An intimate fine-dining restaurant in the French Quarter, serving global-modern cuisine and world flavors inspired by Chef Boswell's Louisiana roots.

RESTAURANTSTELLA.COM

Stanley

A casual counterpart to Stella, serving classic New Orleans comfort food with a unique twist; food that Chef Boswell not only loves to cook, but enjoys himself.

STANLEYRESTAURANT.COM

Scott Boswell
ENTERPRISES

──── CONTACT ────

Rachel Hinton
Director, Public Relations & Private Events
rhinton@chefscottboswell.com

──── ADDRESS ────

547 Saint Ann Street
New Orleans, Louisiana 70116

──── TELEPHONE ────

phone .... (225) 936.7203
fax .... (504) 587.0092

──── WEB ────

chefscottboswell.com

DESIGN FIRM 3 Advertising
ART DIRECTOR Sam Maclay
DESIGNER Tim McGrath
CLIENT The Gutter

DESIGN FIRM 3 Advertising
ART DIRECTOR Sam Maclay
DESIGNER Tim McGrath
CLIENT Day One

DESIGN FIRM 3 Advertising
ART DIRECTOR Sam Maclay
DESIGNER Tim McGrath
CLIENT Alone and Unafraid

DESIGN FIRM 4th Avenue Media
ART DIRECTOR Lucas Mack
DESIGNER Ryne Hill
CLIENT Sealed Mindset

Masculine

MONOGRAMMATIC

Emphasizing a letter or number

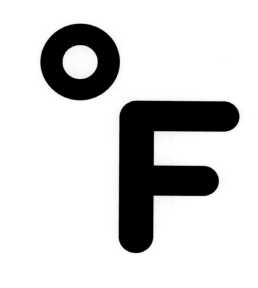

Judges' Selection: Best In Category

Steve Frost is a hard working, no-frills photographer free of pretentiousness or ego.
This logo captures that personality well, and adds the memorable twist of using
a stylized Fahrenheit symbol to underscore the frosty nature of his surname.

DESIGN FIRM Zync   **DESIGNER** Marko Zonta   **CLIENT** Frost Photo

DESIGN FIRM   Archrival
ART DIRECTOR   Clint! Runge
DESIGNER   Joel Kreutzer
CLIENT   Sòlas Distillery

DESIGN FIRM   Alphabet Arm Design
ART DIRECTOR   Aaron Belyea
DESIGNER   Ryan Frease
CLIENT   Haycon

DESIGN FIRM   Bruketa&Zinic OM
ART DIRECTORS   Imelda Ramovic
Mirel Hadzijusufovic
Davor Bruketa
Nikola Zinic
DESIGNERS   Imelda Ramovic
Mirel Hadzijusufovic
CLIENT   Cromaris

DESIGN FIRM   Chris Trivizas | Design
DESIGNER   Chris Trivizas
CLIENT   Vrionis SA

DESIGN FIRM Archrival   **ART DIRECTOR** Clint! Runge   **DESIGNER** Joel Kreutzer   **CLIENT** Sòlas Distillery

FROST PHOTO
25 PENNINGTON CRESCENT
GEORGETOWN, ON L7G 4L2
P 905.877.4385 C 416.567.4099

STEVE@**FROSTPHOTO.CA**

°F

DESIGN FIRM Zync   **ART DIRECTOR** Marko Zonta   **DESIGNER** Lee Boulden   **CLIENT** Frost Photo

FROST PHOTO
25 PENNINGTON CRESCENT
GEORGETOWN ON L7G 4L3
P 905.877.4385 C 416.567.4299
STEVE@FROSTPHOTO.CA

STEVE FROST

°F

DESIGN FIRM Carol McLeod Design **ART DIRECTOR** Carol McLeod **DESIGNER** Chris Daigneault **CLIENT** Carol McLeod Design

DESIGN FIRM   Drexler
DESIGNER   Matt Coleman
CLIENT   Renbarger Tech Services

DESIGN FIRM   Design Center of Michigan State University
ART DIRECTOR Chris Corneal
DESIGNER   Cory Pitzer
CLIENT   Department of Philosophy
              Michigan State University

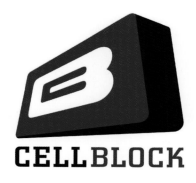

DESIGN FIRM   Extra Crispy Creative
DESIGNER   Paul Mitchell
CLIENT   Cell Block

DESIGN FIRM   Flight Deck Creative
DESIGNER   Jason Rahn
CLIENT   Treasure Chest

DESIGN FIRM Miles Design **DESIGNER** Josh Miles **CLIENT** Miles Design

DESIGN FIRM   Grade Design Consultants
DESIGNER   Paul Palmer-Edwards
CLIENT   Elephant Book Company

DESIGN FIRM   Giorgio Davanzo Design
DESIGNER   Giorgio Davanzo
CLIENT   Fiori Chocolate

FIORICHOCOLATE

twelve south

DESIGN FIRM   HOOK
DESIGNER   Brady Waggoner
CLIENT   twelve south

DESIGN FIRM   Jeremy Slagle Graphic Design
DESIGNER   Jeremy Slagle
CLIENT   Jeremy Slagle Graphic Design

Monogrammatic

DESIGN FIRM KEVIN AKERS design + imagery
DESIGNER Kevin Akers
CLIENT G-4 Developers

DESIGN FIRM Lloyd's Graphic Design Ltd
DESIGNER Alexander Lloyd
CLIENT David James Tree Services

DESIGN FIRM Mirko Ilić Corp.
ART DIRECTOR Mirko Ilić
DESIGNERS Mirko Ilić
Jee-eun Lee
CLIENT Richfield Hospitality

DESIGN FIRM Niedermeier Design
DESIGNER Kurt Niedermeier
CLIENT Khunu

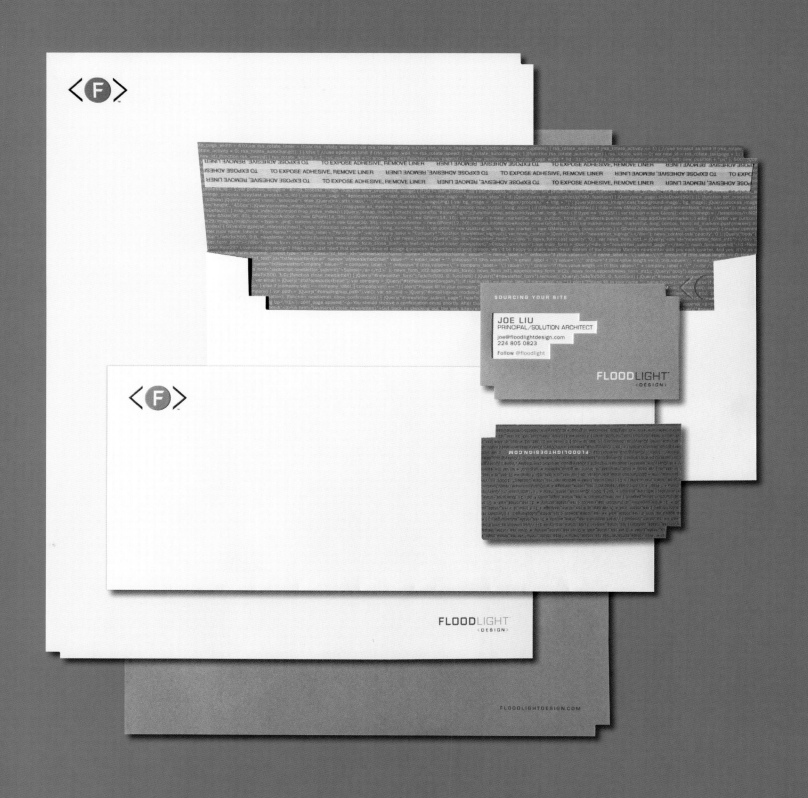

DESIGN FIRM Rule29 Creative **ART DIRECTOR** Justin Ahrens **DESIGNER** Tim Damitz **CLIENT** Floodlight Design

DESIGN FIRM   Owen Jones Design
DESIGNER   Owen Jones
CLIENT   Graceworks

DESIGN FIRM   Sinclair Art Direction & Design
DESIGNER   Robert Sinclair
CLIENT   Petroglyphs

DESIGN FIRM   Sensus Design Factory
ART DIRECTOR   Nedjeljko Spoljar
DESIGNERS   Nedjeljko Spoljar
  Kristina Spoljar
CLIENT   IGEPA-Plana Papiri Zagreb

DESIGN FIRM   Ten26 Design Group
DESIGNER   Tony Demakis
CLIENT   J.P. Wendt Construction Management

DESIGN FIRM 3 Advertising
ART DIRECTOR Sam Maclay
DESIGNER Tim McGrath
CLIENT F8 Photography

DESIGN FIRM 5Seven
ART DIRECTORS Katherine Filice
Clint Delapaz
DESIGNER Clint Delapaz
CLIENT MBS

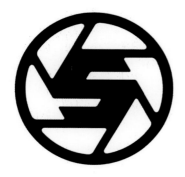

CASS HOLLOWAY & Co

DESIGN FIRM 5Seven
DESIGNER Clint Delapaz
CLIENT Stephen Higgins Photography

DESIGN FIRM 4th Avenue Media
ART DIRECTOR Lucas Mack
DESIGNER Ryne Hill
CLIENT Cass Holloway & Co.

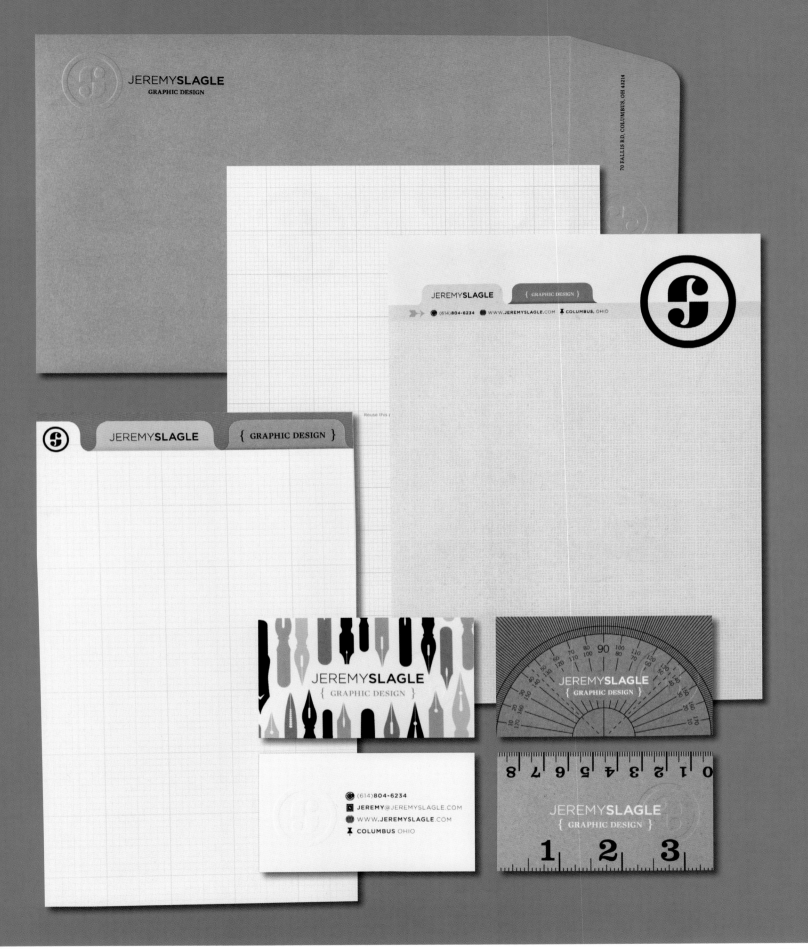

JEREMYSLAGLE
GRAPHIC DESIGN

JEREMYSLAGLE.COM

 (614)804-6234

 JEREMY@JEREMYSLAGLE.COM

WWW.JEREMYSLAGLE.COM

COLUMBUS OHIO

SIMPLE

Less, but lasting

HONOLULU
FILM FESTIVAL

Judges' Selection: Best In Category

Sometimes the simplest solutions are the best ones, as exemplified in this combination
of Hawaii's traditional hibiscus flower with a film reel to represent the Honolulu Film Festival.

DESIGNER Alexander Wende   **CLIENT** Honolulu Film Festival

DESIGNER   Alexander Wende
CLIENT   decorluv

DESIGN FIRM   AkarStudios
ART DIRECTOR   Sat Garg
DESIGNER   Sean W. Morris
CLIENT   Santa Monica Eye Medical Group

DESIGN FIRM   Capsule
ART DIRECTOR   Brian Adducci
DESIGNER   Michelle Hyster
CLIENT   Sightpath Medical

DESIGN FIRM   christiansen : creative
ART DIRECTOR   Tricia Christiansen
DESIGNER   David MacDonald
CLIENT   Osceola Medical Center, Acorn Grill

cantrell+strenski+mehringer LLP
ATTORNEYS AT LAW

cantrell+strenski+mehringer LLP
ATTORNEYS AT LAW

Joannie Saba + Administrator
jsaba@csmlawfirm.com
317 352-3509 Direct

www.**csmlawfirm**.com

2400 Market Tower + 10 West Market Street
Indianapolis, IN 46204
317 352-3500 Main + 317 352-3501 Fax

cantrell+strenski+mehringer LLP
ATTORNEYS AT LAW

2400 Market Tower + 10 West Market Street + Indianapolis, Indiana 46204 + 317 352-3500 Main + 317 352-3501 Fax + www.csmlawfirm.com

VISION│BUILT

armtec

205-26229 Twp Rd. 531A
Acheson AB T7X 5A4
Canada

TEL 780-960-3204
FAX 780-960-2674

info@armtec.com
armtec.com

A.E. CONCRETE
ARMTEC
BOUCHER PRECAST CONCRETE
BROOKLIN CONCRETE
CON-FORCE CONCRETE PRODUCTS
CON-FORCE STRUCTURES
DURISOL
GROUPE TREMCA
PRE-CON

DESIGN FIRM Zync   ART DIRECTOR Marko Zonta   DESIGNER Lee Boulden   CLIENT Armtec

DESIGN FIRM   DEI Creative
ART DIRECTORS Sara Green
              Shannon Palmer
              Sue Dooley
DESIGNER   Andrea Wallace
CLIENT   Airstream

DESIGN FIRM   christiansen : creative
ART DIRECTOR Tricia Christiansen
DESIGNER   David MacDonald
CLIENT   BI

greencentives

green pantry

DESIGN FIRM   Entermotion
DESIGNER   Lea Morrow
CLIENT   Green Pantry

DESIGN FIRM   Entermotion
DESIGNER   Lea Morrow
CLIENT   RXDrugRep.com

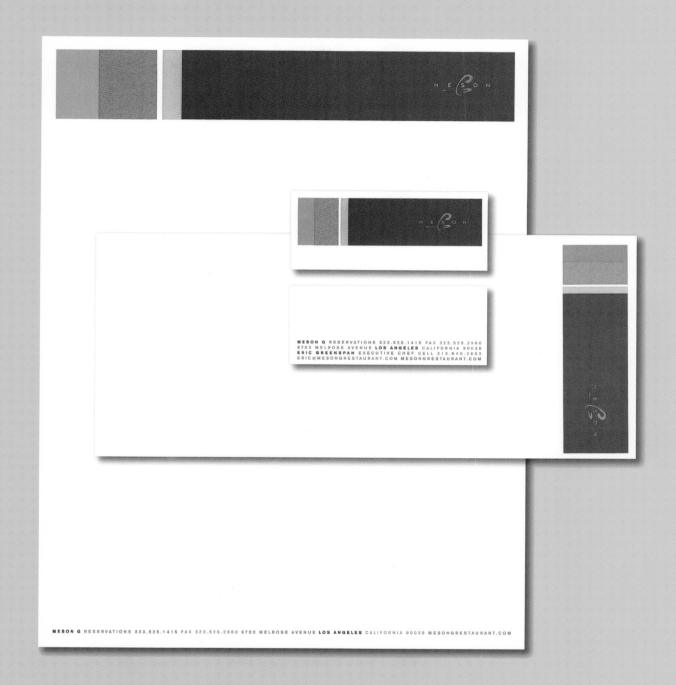

Gregory Moureau
MIGRE BVBA

BROEKSTRAAT 8-13 // 1840 MALDEREN
T. +32 (0)2 262 14 84 // F. +32 (0)2 262 18 14

GREGORY@MIGREMY.BE
WWW.MIGREMY.BE

Lieve Vanderveken
GREMY BVBA

BROEKSTRAAT 8-13 // 1840 MALDEREN
T. +32 (0)2 262 14 84 // F. +32 (0)2 262 18 14

LIEVE@MIGREMY.BE
WWW.MIGREMY.BE

BROEKSTRAAT 8-13 // 1840 MALDEREN
TEL. +32 (0)2 262 14 84 // FAX +32 (0)2 262 18 14
WWW.MIGREMY.BE // INFO@MIGREMY.BE

DESIGN FIRM Chilli Design & Multimedia **DESIGNERS** Frederik Vanderfaeillie, Annelies De Baets **CLIENT** MIGRE - GREMY

DESIGN FIRM Jeremy Slagle Graphic Design
DESIGNER Jeremy Slagle
CLIENT Haring Realty

DESIGN FIRM KEVIN AKERS design + imagery
DESIGNER Kevin Akers
CLIENT Geeper's Peepers Optical Boutique

DESIGN FIRM KEVIN AKERS design + imagery
ART DIRECTOR Kevin Akers
DESIGNERS Kevin Akers
  Kim Ros
CLIENT Jareva Technolgies—Shape Technolgy

DESIGN FIRM KEVIN AKERS design + imagery
DESIGNER Kevin Akers
CLIENT Bay One Technologies/Burson-Marsteller

DESIGN FIRM   Lloyd's Graphic Design Ltd
DESIGNER   Alexander Lloyd
CLIENT   The Dressing Room

DESIGN FIRM   Miriello Grafico
ART DIRECTORS   Ron Miriello
                Tracy Meiners
DESIGNER   Tracy Meiners
CLIENT   Smarter Foods

DESIGN FIRM   P.Berkbigler Design & Illustration
ART DIRECTORS   Paul Berkbigler
                Gretchen Jameson
DESIGNER   Paul Berkbigler
CLIENT   purePR, LLC

DESIGN FIRM   Paragon Marketing Communications
DESIGNER   Konstantin Assenov
CLIENT   Huneidi Group

cultuur · erfgoed · archeologie

CO₇ ARCHEO₇ | Reningelststraat 13 · B-8950 Kemmel

CULTUURDIENST

CO₇

Greet Desodt
Coördinator

Grote Markt 1
B-8970 Poperinge
T +32-(0)57-346 694
M +32-(0)472-937 799
F +32-(0)57-337 581
E coordinator@co7.be
W www.cultuurdienstco7.be

zuurstof voor cultuur

ruimte voor archeologie

CO₇

CO₇ is het samenwerkingsverband voor cultuur, erfgoed en archeologie tussen de gemeenten Heuvelland, Ieper, Langemark-Poelkapelle, Mesen, Poperinge, Vleteren en Zonnebeke.

Maatschappelijke zetel + contactadres:
Stadhuis Poperinge
Grote Markt 1
B-8970 Poperinge
ondernemingsnummer:
0877.372.225

www.co7.be

DESIGN FIRM Design Sense DESIGNER Katelijne De Muelenaere CLIENT CO7

DESIGN FIRM Poccuo
DESIGNERS Mason Kessinger
Phillip Zelnar
CLIENT National Atmospheric Deposition Program

DESIGNER Rashi Ketan Gandhi
CLIENT The Keirtan Foundation

DESIGN FIRM Roskelly Inc.
DESIGNER Thomas Roskelly
CLIENT Mothers of Multiples NH Chapter

DESIGN FIRM Stebbings Partners
CLIENT Tastings Wine Bar & Bistro

clark lara
photography*

*weddings & portraits
tel 832.489.4328 | email clark@clarklaraphotography.com | clarklaraphotography.com

DESIGN FIRM Spindletop Design   DESIGNER Jennifer Blanco   CLIENT Clark Lara Photography

CL **CL**

CL

CL

CL

CL

clark lara
photography*

weddings & portraits

* weddings & portraits
tel 832.489.4328
email clark@clarklarap
clarklaraphotogr

clark lara
photog

DESIGN FIRM That's Nice
DESIGNERS Erin Carney
Nigel Walker
CLIENT My Water

DESIGN FIRM TOKY Branding + Design
ART DIRECTOR Eric Thoelke
DESIGNER Mary Rosamond
CLIENT Messiah Lutheran Church

DESIGN FIRM TOKY Branding + Design
ART DIRECTOR Eric Thoelke
DESIGNER Travis Brown
CLIENT Catholic Health Association
of the United States

DESIGN FIRM Up Inc
ART DIRECTOR Carey George
DESIGNER Mike Nitsopoulos
CLIENT Up Inc

DESIGN FIRM Wing Chan Design, Inc.
ART DIRECTOR Wing Chan
DESIGNERS Lang Xiao
Katarina Tadich
CLIENT ALWAYS Healthcare Organization

DESIGN FIRM 3 Advertising
ART DIRECTOR Sam Maclay
DESIGNER Tim McGrath
CLIENT Medicine in Motion

DESIGN FIRM 3 Advertising
ART DIRECTOR Sam Maclay
DESIGNER Tim McGrath
CLIENT Mortgage Finance Authority

DESIGN FIRM 5Seven
DESIGNER Clint Delapaz
CLIENT Stepping Stone

TYPOGRAPHIC

Building images with type

Judges' Selection: Best In Category

In a testament to the power of simple, typographically based marks,
the Des Moines Playhouse comes to life as the curtain rises in their logo.

DESIGN FIRM Cooper Smith & Company   **ART DIRECTOR** Sally Cooper Smith   **DESIGNERS** Angela Griner, Robin Wasteney   **CLIENT** Des Moines Playhouse

DESIGN FIRM BBM&D Strategic Branding
ART DIRECTOR Barbara Brown
DESIGNER Arrate Garcia
CLIENT Fox & Frank Enterprises

DESIGN FIRM Chris Rooney Illustration/Design
DESIGNER Chris Rooney
CLIENT PlanTed

FOX&FRANK
ENTERPRISES

LAVODKA

DESIGN FIRM CINDERBLOC
DESIGNERS Ryan Di Leo
Michael Nitsopoulos
CLIENT V1 Vodka

DESIGN FIRM Dream On (Paris)
DESIGNER Ivan Grangeon
CLIENT Timm

DESIGN FIRM Believe in Ltd   **DESIGNER** Blair Thomson   **CLIENT** Believe in

Believe in™
design, art direction
& branding

33—35 Southernhay East
Exeter
EX1 1NX
+44 (0)1392 453000
mail@believein.co.uk
www.believein.co.uk

Registered in
England & Wales

Company no.
6259172

VAT no.
679 3421 04

11912 WEST WASHINGTON

boulevard

Los Ang___

Californ___

9006_

OFFICE LINE. 310 255 7995   FACSIMILE. 310 255 7996   WW

NRG

580 HOWARD STREET, SUITE 202   SA

NRG

MEANING IS
deeper through
EXPERIENCE

NRG

JOHN@EXPERIENCE**NRG**.COM
John Zutaut
Chief Financial Officer of **NRG Marketing, LLC**
11912 W. WASHINGTON BLVD. LOS ANGELES, CA 90066
OFFICE LINE. 310 255 7995   FACSIMILE. 310 255 7996
Direct Line. 310 997 0028   *Cellular Line.* 213 840 2707

CREATING MEANING
through
EXPERIENCE

NRG

DESIGN FIRM MINE™   **ART DIRECTOR** Christopher Simmons   **DESIGNERS** Christopher Simmons, Tim Belonax   **CLIENT** NRG Marketing, LLC

DESIGN FIRM Diseño Dos Asociados
ART DIRECTORS Juan Carlos García
             Carlos Rivera
DESIGNER Víctor Martínez
CLIENT Tomeiko

DESIGN FIRM DA Studios
DESIGNER Deanna Alcorn
CLIENT Bravado International Group

DESIGN FIRM Damion Hickman Design, Inc.
ART DIRECTOR Damion Hickman
DESIGNER Leighton Hubbell
CLIENT ZELOS WINES

DESIGN FIRM Drexler
DESIGNER Matt Coleman
CLIENT Beatlab

DESIGN FIRM   Eleven19
ART DIRECTOR   Donovan Beery
DESIGNER   Chris Kelly
CLIENT   Fat Ox

DESIGN FIRM   ghost
DESIGNER   Jenkin Hammond
CLIENT   Dr. Jon Roth, MD

DR JON ROTH | MD

PESCAIA

DESIGN FIRM   Giorgio Davanzo Design
DESIGNER   Giorgio Davanzo
CLIENT   Pescaia

DESIGN FIRM   HOOK
DESIGNER   Brady Waggoner
CLIENT   Chef Ken Vedrinski

FUSE®
DESIGN

FUSE®
DESIGN

Fuse Design
16 Stone Yard
12 Plumptre Street
Lace Market
Nottingham
NG1 1JL

Mob/Tel
07838 240745
0115 9501440

Email/Web
adam@fuse-design.co.uk
www.fuse-design.co.uk

Adam Head
Creative Director

FUSE®
DESIGN

Fuse Design Ltd
16 Stone Yard
12 Plumptre Street
Lace Market
Nottingham
NG1 1JL

Tel
0115 9501440

Email/Web
studio@fuse-design.co.uk
www.fuse-design.co.uk

VAT No. 930 1773 41
Company No. 06269089
Registered in England & Wales

FUSE® DESIGN

Fuse Design
16 Stone Yard
12 Plumptre Street
Lace Market
Nottingham
NG1 1JL

Mob/Tel
07838 240745
0115 9501440

Email/Web
adam@fuse-design.co.uk
www.fuse-design.co.uk

Adam Head
Creative Director

Fuse Design Ltd
16 Stone Yard
12 Plumptre Street
Lace Market
Nottingham
NG1 1JL

Tel
0115 95

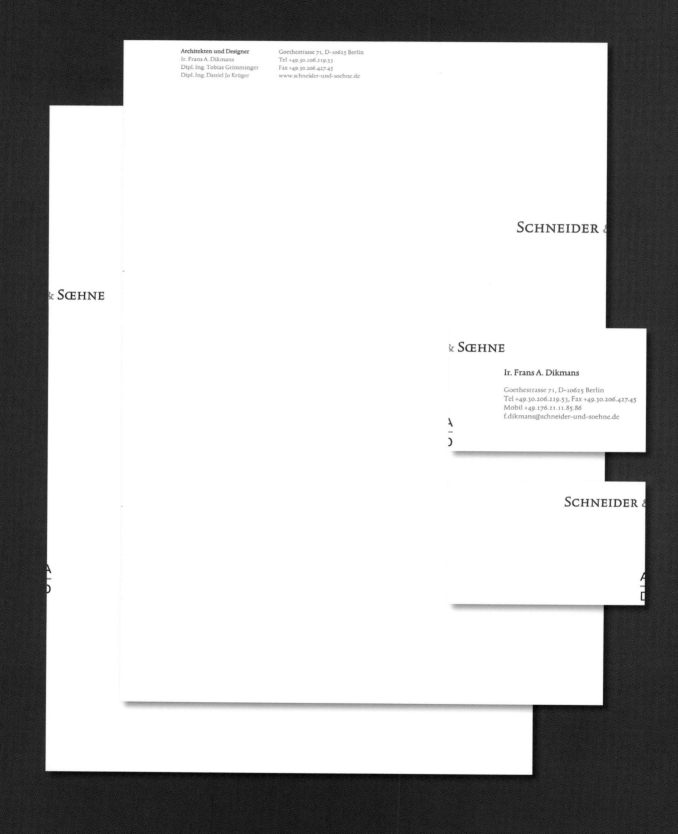

Architekten und Designer
Ir. Frans A. Dikmans
Dipl. Ing. Tobias Grimminger
Dipl. Ing. Daniel Jo Krüger

Goethestrasse 71, D–10625 Berlin
Tel +49.30.206.219.53
Fax +49.30.206.427.45
www.schneider-und-soehne.de

SCHNEIDER &

& SŒHNE

& SŒHNE

Ir. Frans A. Dikmans

Goethestrasse 71, D–10625 Berlin
Tel +49.30.206.219.53, Fax +49.30.206.427.45
Mobil +49.176.21.11.85.86
f.dikmans@schneider-und-soehne.de

SCHNEIDER &

DESIGN FIRM Wanja Ledowski Studio   DESIGNER Wanja Ledowski   CLIENT Schneider & Soehne Architects and Designers

DESIGN FIRM   Kanella
DESIGNER   Kanella Arapoglou
CLIENT   Digenopouloi Bro.

DESIGN FIRM   Keystone Resources
DESIGNER   Rebecca Saldaña
CLIENT   Agency 8

AGENCY

RIVER
SPACE

DESIGN FIRM   Liska + Associates
ART DIRECTOR   Steve Liska
DESIGNER   Liz Johnson
CLIENT   River Space

DESIGN FIRM   Masif_Design Affairs
DESIGNER   Jose Luis Ortiz G.
CLIENT   MopaMopa

Agostoni

North American Sales
8616 La Tijera Boulevard

Suite Number 512
Los Angeles, CA 90045

213.261.0057 Telephone
agostonichocolate.com

th American Sales
La Tijera Boulevard

Suite Number 512
Los Angeles, CA 90045

Kimberly Fox
North American Sales

213.261.0057 Ext. 2 Telephone
323.302.1354 Cellular
310.670.0596 Facsimile
kfox@agostonichocolate.com
8616 La Tijera Boulevard, Suite 512
Los Angeles, California 90045
agostonichocolate.com

Agostoni
Italian Chocolate Since 1946

Agostoni Chocolate Family operated since 1946, we are an Italian modern artisan bean-to-bar producer of premium all natural chocolate for industrial, food service and private label customers. A global leader in organic cocoa processing (5000T+/yr), we secure superior quality fermented cocoa beans (conventional and organic) for our production of cocoa liquor, butter, powder and finished chocolates through an exclusive Equal Partner Direct Buying program, in place in key origins since 1980. Our chocolate making passion: art and science in equal measure.

DESIGN FIRM Ramp Creative + Design   **ART DIRECTOR** Michael Stinson   **DESIGNERS** Oliver Lan, Michael Stinson   **CLIENT** Agostoni Chocolate

DSFM

2300 Yonge Street, Suite 2900   T   416 489 5677
P.O. Box 2384 Toronto Ontario   F   416 489 7794
Canada M4P 1E4   W   condolaw.to

DEACON, SPEARS BARRISTERS
FEDSON +
MONTIZAMBERT SOLICITORS

2300 Yonge Street, Suite 2900
P.O. Box 2384 Toronto Ontario
Canada M4P 1E4

DSFM

condolaw.to

DEACON, SPEARS BARRISTERS
FEDSON +
MONTIZAMBERT SOLICITORS

DEACON, SPEARS BARRISTERS
FEDSON +
MONTIZAMBERT SOLICITORS

Michael J. Campbell LL.B.
Associate
mcampbell@dsfmlaw.com

DSF

416 489 5677 x 305   T   2300 Yonge Street, Suite 2900
416 489 7794   F   P.O. Box 2384 Toronto Ontario
dsfmlaw.com   W   Canada M4P 1E4

DESIGN FIRM CINDERBLOC   **DESIGNERS** Ryan Di Leo, Michael Nitsopoulos   **CLIENT** Deacon, Spears, Fedson + Montizambert: Barristers + Solicitors

DESIGN FIRM   Meta Newhouse Design
DESIGNER   Meta Newhouse
CLIENT   Urnique

DESIGNER   Piotr Karczewski
CLIENT   Pinokio Theatre in Lodz

ÙRNIQUE

pinokio

GRANA PADANO
MANTOVA
449
ULTRA PREMIUM

DESIGNER   Raphael Mahon
CLIENT   Ian Lightfoot Plumber

DESIGN FIRM   Ramp Creative + Design
ART DIRECTOR   Michael Stinson
DESIGNERS   Kristen Williams
Tsz Chan
Oliver Lan
CLIENT   Mantova 449

DESIGN FIRM   Ramp Creative + Design
DESIGNERS   Oliver Lan
Michael Stinson
CLIENT   Agostoni Chocolate

DESIGN FIRM   Trainor Design
DESIGNER   Sarah Lotus Trainor
CLIENT   Beacon Consulting Group

DESIGN FIRM   Wonderwheel Creative
ART DIRECTOR   Tim Merrill
DESIGNER   Sarah Lotus Trainor
CLIENT   Dune Nantucket

DESIGN FIRM   3 Advertising
ART DIRECTOR   Sam Maclay
DESIGNER   Jesse Arneson
CLIENT   New Day

w 5SEVEN.COM

NOTHING SHORT OF CREATIVE

SEVEN

NOTHING SHORT OF CREATIVE

SEVEN

CLINT DELAPAZ
FREELANCE DESIGNER

c 415/385 4521   E CLINT@5SEVEN.COM   w 5SEVEN.COM

NOTHING SHORT OF CREATIVE

SEVEN

NOTHING SHORT OF CREATIVE

SEVEN

DESIGN FIRM 5Seven   **DESIGNER** Clint Delapaz   **CLIENT** 5Seven

WHIMSICAL

Effectively self-aware and spirited

VOGL

GRAFIK
DESIGN

Judges' Selection: Best In Category

Frederiko Vogl's mark is everything a personal logo should be: His surname
is the German word for bird, and he starts each new project with pencil and paper.

DESIGN FIRM Vogl Grafik-Design **DESIGNER** Friederike Vogl **CLIENT** Vogl Grafik-Design

DESIGN FIRM   Agent OX
DESIGNER   Sarah Osborn
CLIENT   Migration Brewing Company

DESIGN FIRM   BrandSavvy, Inc.
DESIGNER   Karl Peters
CLIENT   Chunka Munka Cookie Company

MIGRATION
BREWING CO.

CHUNKA MUNKA
COOKIE COMPANY

DEADLINE
DELIVERY

ZOCALO
TAQUERIA FRESCA
cafe

DESIGN FIRM   Bowhaus Design Groupe
DESIGNER   Matthew T. O'Rourke
CLIENT   DEADLINE DELIVERY

DESIGN FIRM   Chawlie
DESIGNER   Charlie Chauvin
CLIENT   Zocalo Cafe

JOE SCHAAK
PRESIDENT / CREATIVE DIRECTOR

JOE@FIENDCONTENT.COM
● 612 339-8449
● 612 804-8467
119 NORTH 2ND STREET
MINNEAPOLIS, MN 55401

119 NORTH 2ND STREET, MINNEAPOLIS, MN 55401

FIEND INC.

DESIGN FIRM Sussner Design Company   **ART DIRECTOR** Derek Sussner   **DESIGNER** Jamie Paul   **CLIENT** Fiend, Inc.

FIEND INC.
CONTENT CREATION

JOE SCHAAK
PRESIDENT / CREATIVE DIRECTOR

JOE
o 61
d 612

119 NORT
MINNEAP

DESIGN FIRM   Design Nut
DESIGNER   Brent Almond
CLIENT   The Gay Men's Chorus of Washington DC

DESIGN FIRM   Diseño Dos Asociados
ART DIRECTOR   Juan Carlos García
DESIGNER   Carlos Rivera
CLIENT   Global Mystery Shopping

DESIGN FIRM   Grandpa-George Design and Interactive
DESIGNER   Douglas Brull
CLIENT   Coalition Against Toxic Toys

DESIGN FIRM   J Fletcher Design
DESIGNER   Jay Fletcher
CLIENT   Overboard Cocktail Sauce

360° imagery

Stuart Thorp BSc (Hons) MRICS Dip Surv (CEM)

T 0845 8726442   E info@360imagery.co.uk
M 07816 839750   W 360imagery.co.uk

57 Main Street, Barton under Needwood, Staffordshire DE13 8AB

360° imagery

T 0845 8726442   E info@360imagery.co.uk   W 360imagery.co.uk
With Compliments 57 Main Street, Barton under Needwood, Staffordshire DE13 8AB

360° imagery

T 0845 8726442   E info@360imagery.co.uk   W 360imagery.co.uk
57 Main Street, Barton under Needwood, Staffordshire DE13 8AB

360° imagery

DESIGN FIRM Burnthebook   DESIGNER Simon Duckworth   CLIENT 360 Imagery

cutey booty

cutey booty
angie medlock
angie@thecuteybooty.com
1440 ben sawyer blvd. ste. 1101
box 215 mt. pleasant, sc 29464
888.924.9229   888.642.9222
thecuteybooty.com
basic to brilliant

cutey booty
basic to brilliant

cutey booty
basic to brilliant

a gift for you
redeem this card at www.thecuteybooty.com
or by calling 888.924.9229

gift code   amount
cutey booty™
basic to brilliant

DESIGN FIRM Stitch Design Co. **DESIGNERS** Amy Pastre, Courtney Rowson **CLIENT** Cutey Booty

DESIGN FIRM KEVIN AKERS design + imagery
DESIGNER Kevin Akers
CLIENT Jack Lemmon Invitational Golf Tournament

DESIGN FIRM Lizza's Room
DESIGNER Lizza Gutierrez
CLIENT JJ and Cres Yulo

cres yulo
PHOTO GAL

jj yulo
FOOD GUY

DESIGN FIRM Lloyd's Graphic Design Ltd
DESIGNER Alexander Lloyd
CLIENT Skoff

DESIGN FIRM MINE™
ART DIRECTOR Christopher Simmons
DESIGNERS Christopher Simmons
Ty Wilkins
CLIENT Peachpit Press

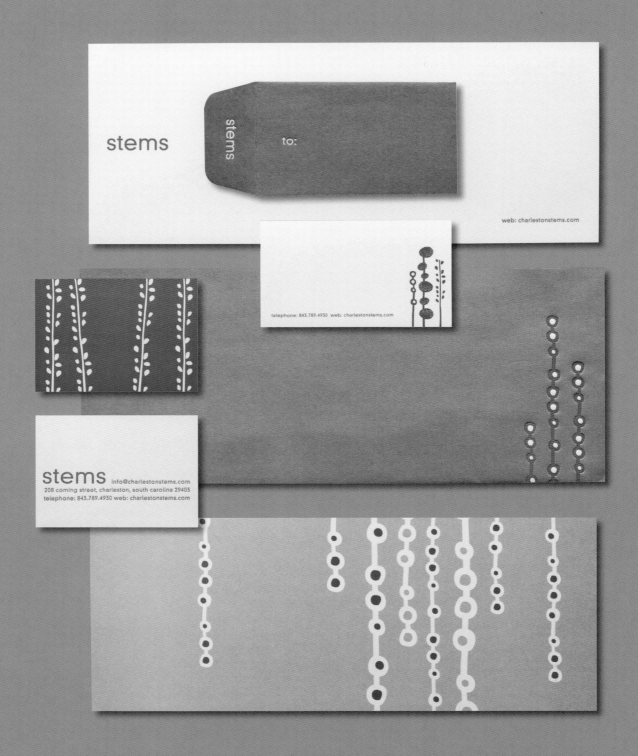

DESIGN FIRM Stitch Design Co. **DESIGNERS** Amy Pastre, Courtney Rowson **CLIENT** Stems

DESIGN FIRM MINE™
ART DIRECTOR Christopher Simmons
DESIGNERS Christopher Simmons
Tim Belonax
CLIENT House of Air

DESIGN FIRM onetreeink
DESIGNER Marcos Calamato
CLIENT Squeeze It!

DESIGN FIRM onetreeink
DESIGNER Marcos Calamato
CLIENT Abducted Studios

DESIGN FIRM ping-pong Design
ART DIRECTORS Barry de Bruin
Maarten Jurriaanse
DESIGNER Maarten Brandenburg
CLIENT Landmarkt

Whimsical

DESIGN FIRM Rome & Gold Creative
ART DIRECTOR Lorenzo Romero
DESIGNER Carlos Bobadilla
CLIENT Karbon Zero

DESIGN FIRM Rome & Gold Creative
ART DIRCTOR Lorenzo Romero
DESIGNERS Lorenzo Romero
Carlos Bobadilla
CLIENT Damage Control Mouthguards

FoodShed

EST 2009

DESIGN FIRM Scout & Co.
DESIGNER Erica Hassinger
CLIENT FoodShed

DESIGN FIRM Shari Margolin Design
ART DIRECTOR Matthew Crouch
DESIGNER Shari Margolin
CLIENT Cartoon Network

The
GREAT
FARINI

RESTAURANT & BAR

WILLIAM E. GALLAGHER
GENERAL MANAGER/ARBITER OF COOL

22 ONTARIO ST.
PORT HOPE, ON L1A 2Z2
TEL. (905) 885-8999
CELL. (514) 268-3635
WILLIAM.E.GALLAGHER@GMAIL.COM

WWW.THEGREATFARINI.COM

DESIGNER Slavek Svab
CLIENT Skywalkers

DESIGNER Stebbings Partners
CLIENT Rhode Runner

SKYWALKERS

LINDEN HILLS
CO-OP
GROCERY & DELI

DESIGN FIRM Sussner Design Company
ART DIRECTOR Derek Sussner
DESIGNER Brandon Van Liere
CLIENT Linden Hills Coop

DESIGN FIRM Sussner Design Company
ART DIRECTOR Derek Sussner
DESIGNER Jamie Paul
CLIENT Fiend, Inc.

DESIGN FIRM Thermostat
DESIGNER Shawn Rosenberger
CLIENT BigDeal.com

DESIGN FIRM Vogl Grafik-Design
DESIGNER Friederike Vogl
CLIENT Albert Sweers Viehhandel GmbH

DESIGN FIRM WORKtoDATE
DESIGNER Greg Bennett
CLIENT Record Breaking Gifts

DESIGN FIRM Zwally Design
ART DIRECTORS Peggi Nadeau
Scott Nadeau
DESIGNER Peggi Nadeau
CLIENT collect the mouse

Whimsical

ABOUT THE AUTHORS

Founded in 2001 by Drew Davies, Oxide Design Co. is a communications and information design firm.

Davies, along with fellow designers Joe Sparano and Adam Torpin, believes that great design comes from clarifying ideas.

Oxide engages in branding and communications design for a nationwide client base, while simultaneously undertaking user interface and information design projects. Oxide served as part of the core Design For Democracy team that developed a set of national ballot design standards for the U.S. Election Assistance Commission and has been working ever since to help states and counties implement effective election design principles.

To learn more, visit **oxidedesign.com**.

CULTURES EAST

WRIGHT
HOME IMPROVEMENT

Letterhead + Logo Design 12

218   DESIGN FIRM Oxide Design Co.   CLIENT Wright Home Improvement   DESIGN FIRM Oxide Design Co.   CLIENT Pitch Coal-Fire Pizzeria

FILM STREAMS

PO BOX 8485
OMAHA, NE 68108-0485
(402) 933-0259
FILMSTREAMS.ORG

LM AS AN ART FORM · DEVOTED TO THE PRESENTATION AND DISCUSSION OF FILM AS AN ART FORM · DEVOTE

N ART FORM · DEVOTED TO THE PRESENTATION AND DISCUSS

OMAHA'S OWN
NONPROFIT CINEMA
(402) 933-0259
INFO@FILMSTREAMS.ORG

AND DISCUSSION OF FILM AS AN ART FORM · DEVOTED TO TH

CASEY LOGAN
COMMUNICATIONS COORDINATOR
CASEY@FILMSTREAMS.ORG

RUTH SOKOLOF THEATER
1340 MIKE FAHEY STREET
OMAHA NE 68102
FILMSTREAMS.ORG

OMAHA'S OWN
NONPROFIT CINEMA
402.933.0259
FILMSTREAMS.ORG

3916 Farnam Street
Omaha, Nebraska 68131

(402) 344-0168
oxidedesign.com

Oxide Design Co.

Drew Davies   Oxide Design Co.
COMMUNICATIONS AND INFORMATION DESIGN

3916 Farnam Street
Omaha, Nebraska 68131

(402) 344-0168
adam@ oxidedesign.com

Oxide Design Co.

DESIGN FIRM Oxide Design Co.   CLIENT Oxide Design Co.

Drew Davies   Oxide Design Co.
COMMUNICATIONS AND INFORMATION DESIGN

3916 Farnam Street
Omaha, Nebraska 68131

(402) 344-0168
adam@ oxidedesign.com

3916 Farnam Street
Omaha, Nebraska 68131

(402) 344-0168
oxidedesign.com

Oxide Design Co.

Drew Davies   Oxide Design Co.
COMMUNICATIONS AND INFORMATION DESIGN

keen

keen

Keen Guides b. 2008
A-10 Envelope

3300 North Fairfax Drive
Suite No. 208
Arlington, VA 22201

Karen Borchert b. 1978
Chief Executive Officer

202.486.9495
karen@keenguides.org

keen

Keen Guides b. 2008
Letterhead

3300 North Fairfax Drive
Suite No. 208
Arlington, VA 22201
keenguides.org

DESIGN FIRM Oxide Design Co. **CLIENT** Keen Guides

CHRISTMAS
AT UNION STATION

OMMEN
CUSTOM HOMES

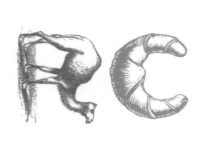

Elizabeth Hare
sensemaker

(917) 721-1346

elizabeth@
readycollective.com

ReadyCollective

word
MADE
flesh

Angelene
Samuel
Project Coordinator

india

angelene.samuel@
wordmadeflesh.org
49/28 Ganapathy
Rao Nagar,
Kolathur, Chennai
600099
91 44 25507231

word
MADE
flesh

Erin Harrell
Field Administrator

word
MADE
flesh

Mandy Mowers
Publications Editor

International Office

marcia.ghali@
wordmadeflesh.org
P.O. Box 70
Omaha, NE 68101
USA
1.800.279.4543

word
MADE
flesh

Phileena
Heuertz
International
Associate Director
of Community Care

india

sarah.lance@
wordmadeflesh.org
P.O. Box 70
Omaha, NE 68101
USA

1.800.279.4543

DESIGN FIRM Oxide Design Co.   **CLIENT** Word Made Flesh

word
MADE
flesh

Angelene
Samuel

Project Coordinat

Publ

Chris
Heue

Internati

Ste
Mc

Serv
Coo

Pa
Off

Jen
Pas

Field

Ma
Sho
Dire
Soci

Phi
He

Inte
Asso
of Communi

N.S.F. 1

ISSUED BY THE NORTH SEA
BOARD OF TRADE.

Note.—Not unlike the process of filmmaking, the North Sea is a constantly shifting and sometimes turbulent adventure. Those sailing its waters are wise in choosing a seasoned crew, setting a true course and trusting their instincts. But even then, successful passage is not ensured. North Sea Films is a veteran navigator of creative voyages, knowing how to master creative crosswinds of water and film alike. No vessel has ever been lost at the hands of their team. Never has a traveler felt the heavy weight of regret for engaging North Sea Films to helm their creative venture. (Sec. 117 of N.S.F. Act, 1894)

OFFICIAL LOG BOOK
AND
ACCOUNT OF VOYAGES AND CREW
OF A VESSEL OF LESS THAN 80 TONS REGISTER
EXCLUSIVELY EMPLOYED IN THE WATERS OF THE NORTH SEA.

Inventory of Cargo, to be here stated. Note—To be filled in by the Shipping Master.

Remarks on this voyage or cargo thereof, report directly on this Log.
For additional parcels, include appropriate Addendum. (N.S.F. A1, A2, etc.)

Correspondence.	PARCELS REQUIRING AN ADDENDUM.	
Proposal for Future Services.	CD.	DVD.
Invoice for Services Rendered.	Tape.	Film.

Date.	Shipper.		CONSIGNEE		POSITION.
		Name.	Town and Country.		Lat. long.
1 July 2007	North Sea Films	Oxide Design Co.	Omaha, NE		41°26' N W

REMARKS.

N.S.F. 2   North Sea Films, Inc. — 41°15'28"N, 95°57'2"W — 2626 Harney Street — Omaha, Nebraska, 68131

ISSUED BY THE NORTH SEA
BOARD OF TRADE.

CARGO REGISTER
FOR DOCUMENTS AND PARCELS
OF ANY NATURE
BEING CARRIED OVER THE WATERS OF THE NORTH SEA.

CONSIGNEE.	Name.	Drew Davies
	Company.	Oxide Design Co.
	Address.	4013 Farnam St.
	Town & Country.	Omaha, Nebraska 68131

North Sea Films, Incorporated — northseafilms.com
41°15'28"N, 95°57'2"W — 2626 Harney Street — Omaha, Nebraska, 68131 — Telecommunication, 001-402-393-8700 — Telefacsimile, 001-402-393-8762 — wayfare@northseafilms.com

---

N.S.F. 4   CREW
IDENTIFICATION
OF A PERSON EMPLOYED
IN THE WATERS OF THE NORTH SEA.

ISSUED BY THE NORTH SEA
BOARD OF TRADE.

CREW MEMBER SEAL.

I, Dana Altman on board a vessel of the North Sea Films Company,
having an e-mail address of wayfare @northseafilms.com
being the height of 5 feet 11 inches, brown hair,
brown eyes, and aged 40 years, or thereabouts,
do hereby swear to the pursuance of the Laws set forth
by the NORTH SEA BOARD OF TRADE and those of its districts.

North Sea Films, Incorporated — northseafilms.com
41°15'28"N, 95°57'2"W — 2626 Harney Street — Omaha, Nebraska, 68131
Telecommunication, 001-402-393-8700 — Telefacsimile, 001-402-393-8762

Signed. Dana Altman

CONTRIBUTORS

3 Advertising
1550 Mercantile Avenue Northeast
Suite 201
Albuquerque, NM 87107
505.293.2333
3advertising.com
105, 135, 136, 137, 153, 175, 195

3rd Edge
162 Newark Avenue
Jersey City, NJ 07302
201.395.9960
3rdedge.com
73

4th Avenue Media
PO Box 40266
Bellevue, WA 98015
425.454.4442
4thavenuemedia.com
137, 153

5Seven
465 10th Street
Suite 306
San Francisco, CA 94103
415.655.9763
5seven.com
22, 73, 153, 175, 196

10 Associates
6A Cartwright Court
Bradley Business Park
Dyson Wood Way
Huddersfield
HD2 1GN
United Kingdom
148.454.3905
10associates.co.uk
27

A3 Design, Inc.
PO Box 327
Webster, NY 14580
585.542.8303
a3-design.com
26, 71, 122

Agent OX
4614 Northeast 16th Avenue
Portland, OR 97211
612.804.9442
62, 200

AkarStudios
1404 Third Street Promenade
Suite 201
Santa Monica, CA 90401
310.393.0625
akarstudios.com
160

Alexander Wende
Neue Strasse 3
89077 Ulm
Germany
behance.net/alexwende
26, 108, 159

Alphabet Arm Design
500 Harrison Avenue (3R)
Boston, MA 02118
617.451.9990
alphabetarm.com
46, 62, 96, 140

Amy Lewis Design
36 Miller Street
Highett, Victoria
Australia 3190
613.9532.5240
amylewisdesign.com.au
76

anxious frank design
6608 North 110 Avenue
Omaha, NE 68164
402.598.3743
anxiousfrank.com
46

Archrival
720 O Street, Lot A
Lincoln, NE 68508
402.435.2525
archrival.com
96, 140, 141

ATOMICvibe
121 Station North Mews
Baltimore, MD 21202
443.534.6051
atomicvibe.net
126

Bagby & Co.
1430 North Dearborn
Apartment 411
Chicago, IL 60610
717.372.0437
nicolezieglerdesign.com
28

BBM&D Strategic Branding
3 Lincoln Drive
Suite A
Ventura, CA 93001
805.667.6671
bbmd-inc.com
178

Beast Syndicate
PO Box 480093
Charlotte, NC 28269
980.253.3410
12

Bekaert Visual Design Team
Ottergemsesteenweg 334
9000 Gent, Belgium
32 9 329 48 68
johnnybekaert.be
9

Believe in Ltd
33-35 Southernhay East
Exeter, Devon
EX1 1NX
United Kingdom
44 (0) 1392 453000
believein.co.uk
180

Bowhaus Design Groupe
340 North 12th Street
Suite 314
Philadelphia, PA 19107
215.733.0603
bowhausdesign.com
200

brandcut
Morskaya emb 33-125
St. Petersburg, Russia 199155
7 (921) 956-47-23
brandcut.com
12, 26

BrandSavvy, Inc.
8822 South Ridgeline Boulevard
Suite 115
Highlands Ranch, CO 80129
303.471.9991
brandsavvyinc.com
12, 200

Bronson Ma Creative
17706 Copper Sunset
San Antonio, TX 78232
210.767.3135
26

Bruketa&Zinic OM
Zavrtnica 17
Zagreb, Croatia 10 000
385 1 6064 000
bruketa-zinic.com
12, 140

Burnthebook
25 Brunel Parkway. Pride Park.
Derby. DE24 8HR.
United Kingdom
44 (0) 1332 291 200
burnthebook.co.uk
206

CAI Communications
2900 Highwoods Boulevard
Raleigh, NC 27604
919.713.5250
caicommunications.com
15

Capsule
100 2nd Avenue North
Minneapolis, MN 55401
612.341.4525
capsule.us
15, 46, 108, 160

Carol McLeod Design
766 Falmouth Road, D-18
Mashpee, MA 02649
508.477.7482
carolmcleoddesign.com
49, 144

Cathy Solarana Design
3719 South 155th Street
Omaha, NE 68144
402.651.7165
cathysolarana.com
15, 46, 48, 53, 76

CGM Chicago
1141 West Madison Street
Chicago, IL 60607
312.327.5154
cgmchicago.com
35

Chawlie
1004 Juniper
Austin, TX 78702
512.589.0996
chawlie.com
200

Chilli Design + Multimedia
Ketelpoort 9
9000 Gent, Belgium
32 9 223 8539
chilli.be
166

Chris Rooney Illustration/Design
1317 Santa Fe Avenue
Berkeley, CA 94702
415.827.3729
looneyrooney.com
178

Chris Trivizas | Design
161 Sygrou Avenue
Athens, Greece 171 21
30 210 9310803
christrivizas.gr
108, 140

christiansen : creative
511 Second Street
Suite 206
Hudson, WI 54016
715.381.8480
christiansencreative.com
160, 164

CINDERBLOC
192 Spadina Avenue
Suite 106
Toronto, ON Canada M5T 2C2
416.777.BLOC
cinderbloc.com
81, 88, 126, 178, 192

Communication Bureau Proekt
Granatniy Sideway 5
Moscow, Russia 123007
7 (925) 396 11 19
proekt.co.uk
15

Cooper Smith & Company
2820 Bell Avenue
Des Moines, IA 50321
515.244.4133
coopersmithco.com
177

Creative Media
Church House
24 Dublin Road
Omagh, County
Tyrone
BT78 1RY
Northern Ireland
0044 28 8225 5720
creativemediani.com
62, 185

Creative Squall
507 Indian Creek Drive
Trophy Club, TX 76262
214.244.5011
creativesquall.com
40, 49, 51, 113

DA Studios
690 Fifth Street
Suite 213
San Francisco, CA 94107
415.348.8809
dastudios.com
183

Damion Hickman Design, Inc.
26080 Towne Centre Drive
Foothill Ranch, CA 92610
949.916.9888
damionhickman.com
49, 50, 183

DEI Creative
1205 East Pike Street
Suite 2A
Seattle, WA 98122
206.281.4004
deicreative.com
164

**Design Center of Michigan
State University**
26A Kresge Art Center
East Lansing, MI 48820
517.862.2337
art.msu.edu/designcenter
145

Design Nut
3716 Lawrence Avenue
Kensington, MD 20895
301.942.2360
designnut.com
62, 204

Design Sense
Patteelstraat 24
8900 Ypres, Belgium
32 (0) 57 447.665
designsense.be
170

Design Trust
243 26th Street Drive Southeast
Cedar Rapids, IA 52403
319.362.9009
designtrust.net
96

Diseño Dos Asociados
Vía Atlixcáyotl 5208
Torre JV 1, Piso 9-903
Colonia Lomas de Angelópolis
San Andrés Cholula, Puebla
México 72830
52 (222) 431 0110
disenodos.com
101, 107, 113, 183, 204

DogStar Design
626 54th Street South
Birmingham, AL 35212
205.591.2275
dogstardesign.com
81, 96, 113

Dream On (Paris)
21 rue Vauvenargues
75018 Paris
France
33 1 53 84 31 31
dream-on.fr
178

Drexler
1501 St. Paul Street
Suite 123
Baltimore, MD
443.977.4918
drxlr.com
145, 183

EAT Advertising & Design, Inc.
5206 NW Bluff Lane
Parkville, MO 64152
816.505.2950
eatinc.om
81

EIGA Design
Holländische Reihe 31a
22765 Hamburg, Germany
49 40 18 88 123 60
eigadesign.com
18, 113

Eleven19
900 South 74th Plaza
Suite 100
Omaha, NE 68114
402.408.3072
eleven19.com
47, 184

Entermotion Design Studio
105 South Broadway
Suite 800
Wichita, KS 67202
316.264.2277
entermotion.com
31, 50, 164

EXPLORARE
Chinantla # 9. Colonel La Paz
Puebla, Puebla. 72160
México
52 (222) 230 4152
explorare.com
126

Extra Crispy Creative
672 West Lookout Ridge Drive
Suite 202
Washougal, WA 98671
360.771.6340
xcrispy.com
101, 145

Fixation Marketing
4340 East West Highway
Suite 200
Bethesda, MD 20814
240.207.2081
fixation.com
66

Flight Deck Creative
4553 Crooked Ridge
The Colony, TX 75056
214.534.9468
flightdeckcreative.com
18, 95, 101, 145

FreshBrand, LLC
5943 North IPM Drive
Parker, CO 80134
720.771.8881
freshbrand.com
114

Fuel, Inc.
800 North Compton Drive
Hiawatha, IA 52233
319.393.7739
fuel-inc.com
50, 67, 126, 179

Fuse Design
16 Stone Yard
12 Plumptre Street
Nottingham, NG1 1JL
United Kingdom
44 (0) 115 950 1440
fuse-design.co.uk
186

Geyrhalter Design
2525 Main Street
Suite 205
Santa Monica, CA 90405
310.392.7615
geyrhalter.com
114

ghost
929A North Broadway
Oklahoma City, OK 73102
405.605.8147
ghostadv.com
18, 31, 32, 184

Giorgio Davanzo Design
501 Roy Street
Suite 209
Seattle, WA 98109
206.328.5031
davanzodesign.com
147, 184

GoodTwin Design, Inc.
5017 Leavenworth Street #103
Omaha, NE 68106
402.305.1426
good-twin.com
84, 129

Grade Design Consultants
6A Maltings Place
169 Tower Bridge Road
London
SE1 3JB
44 020 7403 1984
gradedesign.com
147

**Grandpa-George Design
and Interactive**
18 North 4th Street
Suite 711
Minneapolis, MN 55401
612.216.5005
grandpa-george.com
204

Hansen Designs
8555 Fairmount Drive
Denver, CO 80247
720.202.1593
jnathanhansen.com
22

HOOK
409 King Street
Floor 4
Charleston, SC 29403
843.853.5532
hookusa.com
66, 125, 147, 184

Ian Ingalls
2041 East Susquehanna Avenue
Philadelphia, PA 19125
215.821.4646
ianingalls.com
123

Insight Design Communications
700 South Marcilene
Wichita, KS 67218
316.262.0085
insightdesign.com
9, 31, 102, 103, 129

INK
9820 Irvine Center Drive
Irvine, CA 92618
949.596.4500
ink-la.com
22

Insight Design Communications
700 South Marcilene
Wichita, KS 67218
316.262.0085
insightdesign.com
9, 31, 102, 103, 129

Insomniac Design Studio
774 North 74th Avenue
Omaha, NE 68114
402.575.7485
insomniacdesignstudio.com
42

J Fletcher Design
287 St. Philip Street
Charleston, SC 29403
843.364.1776
jfletcherdesign.com
50, 84, 114, 204

J. Sayles Design Co.
3701 Beaver Avenue
Des Moines, IA 50310
515.279.2922
saylesdesign.com
97, 103

Janus Marketing Group
Svetogorska 37
11000 Belgrade, Serbia
381.11.3226525
jmg.rs
114, 120

Jarheadesign
125 Dunblaine Avenue
Toronto ON M5M 2S4
Canada
416.780.0776
jarhead.com
120

Jeremy Slagle Graphic Design
70 Fallis Road
Columbus, OH 43214
614.804.6234
jeremyslagle.com
11, 103, 116, 129, 147, 154, 167

John Vingoe
18 Grasslands, Singleton, Ashford,
Kent, TN23 5WN, England
44.(0).778.734.7883
wearerapscallion.co.uk
49

Juicebox Designs
4709 Idaho Avenue
Nashville, TN 37209
615.297.1682
juiceboxdesigns.com
45, 52

Kanella
1-3 Laskoy Street
11 635 Athens Greece
30.210.7656972
kanella.com
84, 120, 189

KAOS Advertising
1110 Brickell Avenue
Suite 804
Miami, FL 33131
305.381.8383
kaosadvertising.com
31

Keely Jackman
Flat 4
21 Queens Avenue
London N10 3PE
44.0791.719.8979
keelyjackman.co.uk
34

KEVIN AKERS Design + Imagery
4095 Lilac Ridge Road
San Ramon, CA 94582
925.735.1015
kevinakers.com
53, 84, 120, 148, 167, 209

Keystone Resources
1329 Nicholson Street
Houston, TX 77008
713.874.0162
keystone-resources.com
189

Kindred Design Studio
757 Shelburne Falls Road
Suite B
Hinesburg, VT 045461
802.482.5535
kindredesign.com
103

Kutchibok
Unit 5, Royal Stuart Workshops,
Adelaide Place, Cardiff Bay,
Cardiff, CF10 5BR
Wales / United Kingdom
44.(0).29.2048.3863
kutchibok.co.uk
80

Limelight Advertising & Design
26 Ontario Street
Suite 200
Port Hope, ON L1A 2T6
Canada
905.885.9895
limelight.org
24

Liska + Associates
Studio 2B
360 West Superior Street
Chicago, IL 60654
312.867.1111
liska.com
189

Lizza's Room
12 Samar Avenue
Quezon City 1103
Philippines
632.927.2778
lizzasroom.com
209

Lloyd's Graphic Design Ltd
17 Westhaven Place
Blenheim 7201 Marlborough
New Zealand
64 3 578 6955
lloydsgraphicdesign.wordpress.com
30, 34, 53, 66, 85, 146, 168, 209

Sarah Lowe
2118 Fisher Place
Knoxville, TN 37920
slowe@utk.edu
865.573.2066
38

Luke Despatie & The Design Firm
292 Ridout Street
Port Hope, ON L1A 1P7
Canada
416.995.0243
thedesignfirm.ca
53, 72, 85, 213

Mad Dog Graphx
1443 West Northern Lights Boulevard
Suite U
Anchorage, AK 99503
907.276.5062
thedogpack.com
56

Masif_Design Affairs
Calle 11b N 36b - 65 / 901
Medellin, Colombia
312.8860
ilovemasif.com
34, 189

Melissa Wehrman Design
10738 Brexton Court
Whitehouse, OH 43571
617.817.2799
melissawehrman.com
85

Meta Newhouse Design
8373 Overlook
Bozeman, MT 59715
406.600.6532
metanewhouse.com
194

Miles Design
9229 Delegates Row
Suite 460
Indianapolis, IN 46240
317.915.8693
milesdesign.com
14, 16, 77, 100, 115, 146, 149, 161

MINE™
190 Putnam Street
San Francisco, CA 94110
415.647.6463
minesf.com
38, 119, 182, 209, 211

Miriello Grafico
1660 Logan Avenue
San Diego, CA 92116
619.234.1124
miriellografico.com
34, 69, 168

Mirko Ilić Corp.
207 East 32nd Street
New York, NY 10016
212.481.9737
mirkoilic.com
21, 118, 148

modern8
145 West 200 South
Salt Lake City, UT 84101
801.355.9541
modern8.com
20, 22

Nicholas Burroughs
19942 Concord Loop
Council Bluffs, IA 51503
402.740.8041
nicholasburroughs.com
39

Niedermeier Design
5943 44th Avenue Southwest
Seattle, WA 98136
206.351.3927
kngraphicdesign.com
23, 119, 121, 148

One Man's Studio
1207 Vine Street, Unit I
Cincinnati, OH 45202
513.479.1656
onemansstudio.com
85

onetreeink
676 Gail Avenue H26
Sunnyvale, CA
408.515.9678
onetreeink.com
121, 211

Owen Jones Design
33 Lincoln Avenue
Plymouth
Devon PL4 7NT
United Kingdom
44.7772.560036
owenjonesdesign.com
121, 152

P.Berkbigler Design & Illustration
2217 A Street
Lincoln, NE 68502
618.593.7107
behance.net/PaulBerkbigler/Frame
168

p11creative
20331 Irvine Avenue Suite 5
Newport Beach, CA 92660
714.641.2090
p11.com
121

Paragon Marketing Communications
PO Box 6097
Salmiya 22071 Kuwait
965.257.16063
paragonmc.com
21, 110, 168

Pavone
1006 Market Street
Harrisburg, PA 17101
717.234.8886
pavone.net
38

People Design
648 Monroe Avenue Northwest
Suite 212
Grand Rapids, MI 49503
616.459.4444
peopledesign.com
13, 21

ping-pong Design
Headoffice NL:
Havenstraat 23a
3024 SG Rotterdam
The Netherlands
31.(0).104365744
pingpongdesign.com
211

Piotr Karczewski
Al. Wyszynskiego 43 m 3
94-047 Lodz, Poland
48.601.897.074
piotrkarczewski.com
194

Pluck™ The Division of Graphic Perception & Design Research
1737 East Lagoon Circle
Clearwater, FL 33765
727.386.8663
sethlevy.com
90, 123

Poccuo
1724 20th Street Northwest
Suite 001
Washington, DC 20009
202.550.3195
poccuo.com
171

Ramp Creative + Design
411 South Main Street
Suite 615
Los Angeles CA 90013
213.623.7267
rampcreative.com
56, 68, 165, 190, 194, 195

Raphael Mahon
19 Dane Bank Road
Northwich, Cheshire
CW9 5PL
United Kingdom
44.7965.584847
ralphmahon.co.uk
194

Rare Method
165 South Main Street
Suite 300
Salt Lake City, UT 84111
801.539.1818
raremethod.com
82

Rashi Gandhi
2015 Chitrakut
Sion Sindhi Colony
Sion [West]
Mumbai - 400022
Maharashtra
India
91.22.24093977
rashigandhi.com
174

RDQLUS Creative
7701 Pierce Street, #4
Omaha, NE 68124
402.212.0108
rdqlus.com
59

Red Eye Graphic Design
6705 South 116th Street
Omaha, NE 68137
402.597.0813
redeyegraphicdesign.com
105

Rhythm Behavior
7331 Landscape Station
Berkeley, CA 94707
510.552.5567
rhythmbehavior.com
69

Rome & Gold Creative
900 Park Avenue Southwest
Suite 201
Albuquerque, NM 87102
505.897.0870
rgcreative.com
212

Root Studio
Root Studio, The Terrace,
Grantham Street, Lincoln, LN2 1BD
United Kingdom
44.1522.528246
rootstudio.co.uk
57

Roskelly Inc.
53 Madison Way
Portsmouth, RI 02871
401.683.5091
roskelly.com
171

Rule29 Creative
501 Hamilton Street
Geneva, IL 60134
630.262.1009
rule29.com
38, 56, 90, 130, 150

Scout & Co.
1550 North Blandena Street
Portland, OR 97217
503.449.5450
scoutandco.com
212

Sensus Design Factory
Nedjeljko Spoljar
Sijecanjska 9
HR-10000 Zagreb
Croatia
385.1.3049010
sensusdesignfactory.com
152

Shari Margolin Design
94 Wyman Street Southeast
Atlanta, GA 30317
404.401.3329
sharimargolin.com
56, 212

Signal, Inc.
1123 Zonilite Road Northeast
Suite E
Atlanta, GA 30306
404.873.6450
signaldesign.com
205

Sinclair Art Direction & Design
542 Brannan Street
Suite 103
San Francisco, CA 94107
415.308.9595
robertsinclair.net
152

Slavek Svab
Vaclavkova 176/2
160 00 Prague 6
Czech Republic
420.602347046
214

Spindletop Design
32222 Tamina Road
Suite F1
Magnolia, TX 77354
347.743.7621
spindletopdesign.com
172

Spur Design
3504 Ash Street
Baltimore, MD 21211
410.235.7803
spurdesign.com
54

Stebbings Partners
427 John L Dietsch Boulevard
Attleboro Falls, MA 02763
508.699.7899
stebbings.com
69, 70, 90, 123, 130, 171, 214

Stitch Design Co.
9 Cannon Street
Charleston, SC 29403
843.722.6296
stitchdesignco.com
9, 58, 59, 61, 64, 78, 86, 91, 92, 104,
127, 128, 130, 169, 201, 208, 210

Studio Cream Design
Studio 211, 166 Glebe Point Road,
Glebe NSW 2037
Australia
61.2.9660.0909
studiocreamdesign.com.au
70, 91

Studio928
223 Cypress Court
Andover, KS 67002
316.210.2799
studio928.com
70

Sussner Design Co.
212 3rd Avenue North
Suite 505
Minneapolis, MN 55401
612.339.2886
sussner.com
98, 105, 131, 202, 214

Ten26 Design Group
Ten26 Design Group
432 Diamando Street
Crystal Lake, IL 60012
847.650.3282
ten26design.com
152

Tenfold Collective
202 East 4th Street
Loveland, CO 80537
970.744.4221
tenfoldcollective.com
63, 130, 134

That's Nice LLC
6 West 20th Street
Floor 3
New York , NY 10011
212.366.4455
thatsnice.com
174

The Creative Method
Studio 10
50 Reservoir Street
Surry Hills, NSW, 2010
Australia
612.8231.9977
thecreativemethod.com
36

The Infantree
21 North Prince Street
Lancaster, PA 17603
717.394.6932
theinfantree.com
39, 109

The O Group
259 West 30th Street
11th Floor
New York, NY 10001
212.398.0100
ogroup.net
75

The Pink Orange LLC
1079 Teviot Road
Schenectady, NY 12308
518.320.8417
thepinkorange.com
90

Thermostat
800 Delaware Street
Berkeley, CA 94710
510.644.3333
youaregettingwarmer.com
215

Tiffany Chen Design
682 Mayland Avenue Southwest
Atlanta, GA 30310
404.353.4909
tiffanymchen.com
123

TOKY Branding + Design
3001 Locust Street
2nd Floor
St. Louis, MO 63103
314.534.2000
toky.com
112, 134, 174

Tom Varisco Designs
608 Baronne Street
New Orleans, LA 70113
504.410.2888
tomvariscodesigns.com
59

Trainor Design
49 Orient Avenue
Arlington, MA 02474
781.643.2283
trainor-design.com
195

Up Inc.
488 Wellington Street West
Suite 302
Toronto, ON
Canada M5V 1E3
416.703.9142
upinc.ca
91, 174

Visual Heroes
Straatweg 19a
3603 CV Maarssen
The Netherlands
31.(0).346.55.71.68
visualheroes.nl
19

Vogl Grafik-Design
Schickstrasse 4
70182 Stuttgart
Germany
49.(0).711.50422828
vogl-grafik.de
199, 215

Wanja Ledowski STUDIO
08 Rue du Chateau Landon
75010 Paris
France
0033.(0).6.73.48.94 71
wanjaledowski.com
39, 188

What Cheer, Inc.
1111 North 13th Street, #106
Omaha, NE 68102
402.943.9768
what-cheer.com
59

Wing Chan Design, Inc.
167 Perry Street
Suite 5C
New York, NY 10014
212.727.9109
wingchandesign.com
73, 175

Wonderwheel Creative
PO Box 2523
Nantucket, MA 02584
508.901.1874
wonderwheelcreative.com
73, 195

WORKtoDATE
39 Rebecca Lane
York, PA 17403
717.683.5712
worktodate.com
91, 132, 215

Yona Lee Design
Avenue de la Gare, 10
CH-1003 Lausanne
Switzerland
41.078.859.7878
yonalee.com
21

Zwally Design
5849 Lemon Street
East Petersburg, PA 17520
717.581.0982
zwallydesign.com
215

Zync
228 Richmond Street East
Suite 200
Toronto, ON
Canada
M5A 1P4
416.322.2865
zync.ca
39, 139, 142, 162

SPECIAL THANKS TO

Elisa Davies
Miles Davies
David & Susan Davies
Betty Sparano
Gina Torpin
Paul & Valli Torpin
Rosie & Glady
Justin Ahrens
Taco John
Herman Miller
Sunset House
Ole Kirk Christiansen
Jim Henson
LuthorCorp
Don Draper
Jacques-Yves Cousteau

Emily Potts and the team at Rockport
and everyone who submitted their design
work for this publication